IT'S BEYOND TECHNOLOGY

By Nancy Dobson

IT'S BEYOND TECHNOLOGY

Nancy Dobson
P.O. Box 71132
Bethesda, Maryland 20813

Other books by Nancy Dobson --In print:

99 Lyrics by Nancy Dobson

Catching Curves, a poetic commentary on the scriptures

Knocking On God's Door

Singing the Psalms

SOUL Question

The Gospel's Message Within The Message

The Torah Conscious Christian, Biblical Law by subject, paraphrased, with commentary

The Torah Conscious Christian's Guide To Holy Days

What the Spirit Sees....

Only on Kindle:

If You Ask Me....

If you would like to order copies you would key the whole title into a search window and, if the title doesn't come up, add "by Nancy Dobson."

TABLE OF CONTENTS

INTRODUCTION

You prepare for what comes next after childhood by learning a trade or a profession. You prepare for what comes next after retirement by investing wisely and saving some assets aside. You also prepare for what comes next after material life – for your life as it continues in the spiritual realm.

Oh, you think there is no spiritual realm. What if you're wrong? Remember those who have had near death experiences and testified that they were aware while on the other side of life. And don't forget the many who have experienced communication from a loved one who has died. Better think again.

Oh, you think Jesus did it all for you and you can live however you want while here and still be happy and carefree in the spiritual realm. That isn't what Jesus taught. Jesus taught accountability, judgment and *how to prepare* for life in the spiritual realm.

It is easier than you think to prepare for what comes next after this life, and by preparing for that you make this life better as well.

While we use technology to provide some conveniences for us in our current life, technology cannot help us prepare for what comes next after this life. To prepare for what comes next, we not only have to develop the spiritual sensitivity to perceive God's daily guidance, but we have to exercise with spiritual disciplines to build strengths and avoid stumbling as we face the inevitable challenges of our current ever-changing social and material environments. Technology can't help us with this. The ways we develop spiritual sensitivity and strength are beyond technology.

PEARL OF GREAT PRICE

When I was about five years old my mother told me about her older sister who had died when she was a teenager. She said that just before she died her sister said she saw angels and they were beautiful and she was going to go and be with them. Then my mother put me down for a nap and her parting words were, "Well, the good die young." I spent the rest of that day wondering why I wasn't dead – because I thought I was good, or at least I tried to be.

As a result, I see death both ways. While it is obvious that people are sad to not be able to interact with a loved one who is gone, and their dreams for that person's future have disappeared, I also think of death as a reward. If you are good enough, you get to go and be with God.

If it is so good to be with God, some might want to skip the many pressures and challenges of living on Earth and hasten their entrance to the spiritual realm. However, the spiritual consequences of suicide – whether deliberate or through deliberate carelessness – are extremely harsh. Those who throw the gift of life back in God's face are not rewarded. We must respect this God-given opportunity and all those who have supported and nurtured us through life. We are in this realm for the purpose of learning and developing spiritually and we are meant to drain every drop of spiritual learning from the cup before we leave.

Everyone is born with their own unique abilities. The reason we are here is to use our abilities to engage with the challenges of life and, by doing so, to increase our knowledge, skills and strengths. If we run away from life's challenges, we waste a precious opportunity to grow, and we end up with even less ability than we started with, since abilities not used atrophy. (Luke 19:11-26).

Jesus told a story about a man who discovered a pearl of great price and gave everything he had so he could own that pearl.

(Matthew 13:45-46) Pearls are formed inside of oysters. A piece of grit gets inside an oyster and it irritates the oyster. So, the oyster responds by rubbing against the grit, again and again and again until it creates a smooth, hard covering all around that piece of grit. That covering is a pearl. The symbolism means that working with whatever irritates and challenges us and learning lessons from the injustice, the illogic and the difficulties of life while employing the laws of spiritual nature, gives us something priceless to take with us – and the only thing we can take with us – when we enter the spiritual realm after our death here.

There is another reason for suicide besides fear of the future, and that is depression. If you are constantly depressed, or if you have experienced a tragedy, talk with a professional counselor, your religious teachers, your family or your friends. They'll be glad to comfort you, and may offer enlightening observations and expert advice. Reaching out to help others is another way to overcome depression. When you are helping others you have less time to dwell on your own problems. Reading inspirational literature and listening to uplifting music also help counter depression.

In addition, some depression is caused by body chemistry. Scientists have learned that artificial flavorings cause depression. It is an easy thing to simply read ingredients labels and avoid foods that have artificial flavorings. Choosing against other artificial ingredients also will help you manage your emotions. After you learn safe recipes and the brands of your favorite foods, grocery shopping is quick and easy. Then you only need to take a few seconds to check ingredients for any new food or drink you want to try.

It is in the process of working towards our goals that we develop layers of patience, humility, compassion, loyalty, wisdom, strength and endurance in the invisible part of ourselves – the pearl of great price. Achieving a goal is nice, but just making an honest effort also creates something priceless and precious that is yours for eternity. And that in itself is worth engaging with all the challenges that life offers.

WHY WE?

Charles M. Schulz wrote a comic strip called *Peanuts*. In one segment the character Charlie Brown concluded that the purpose of life is to make people happy. Then he realized, "I'm not happy. SO, SOMEBODY ISN'T DOING HIS JOB!"

Some people think that it is God's job to make us happy. So, when they encounter challenges in life, they think God is falling down on His job. The problem, of course, is to better understand who we are and why we are here. Then we might discover what the Designer and Creator of the spiritual and material realms wants of us. What is our job, and what is God's agenda?

How did we, who are so different from every other animal on Earth, come to be in the material realm? Physicists tell us that matter is condensed energy. Because we are eternal spirits (a type of energy) we might consider that we caused ourselves to condense into material forms. How? The Abrahamic religions teach that souls who are on Earth are those who rebelled against God and chose their will over God's will. This rebellion caused us to condense into matter. Therefore, since we chose materiality, we are ultimately responsible for the challenges we face while we are in the material realm. Nevertheless, we have the power to again choose God's will over our own and return to where we were before.

While we are subject to the repercussions of having chosen our will over our Creator's, God has never left us. In fact, God created a venue where we can continue to choose our own will until we recognize that choosing God's will is better. God has waited patiently for us to recognize our errors and return to being obedient to God so we may prepare to return to our safe and wondrous place that is beyond time and substance.

Like the unruly student who has to sit outside the classroom, everyone on Earth is here in "time out" because we have chosen our will over God's will. God's agenda is for us to return to the wonders and safety of God's place and to escape the insecurities, stresses and sadness common in the material realm. While we may be focused on pursuing material things that we think will make us happy, God is focused on guiding us to become aware of and choose that which will bring us eternal happiness.

God isn't a genie of Whom we can demand the fulfillment of all our material desires. Instead, the omnipotent, omniscient Creator of laws for both the material and spiritual realms desires that each soul on Earth have eternal peace and bliss and be fully restored to our place in God's kingdom from which we came – which, we eventually realize, is also our own deepest spiritual desire.

Therefore, it is everyone's job to learn a little more each day about their own living spirit – its strengths and weaknesses, the type of spiritual food it needs to be healthy, what to avoid that is dangerous to spiritual health, how to use the spirit to perceive God's guidance, how to build its strengths to pursue the missions to which God leads us and how to choose what is of eternal spiritual value over what is of passing material desire.

For us to achieve God's (and our) desire that we return to God's place, we must first acknowledge the reason we are here. Repentance means confession and a changed life. After his resurrection, Jesus told his disciples to go to all nations and teach repentance for the forgiveness of sins. (Luke 24:46-47) When we repent we try to change our habits. God can help us work through the many tests that come to us while we seek to change our lives – if we develop spiritual sensitivity so we are able to perceive God's ready guidance.

The Psalmist says there is nowhere that God is not and that God never sleeps but is always with us. All we have to do is ask for God's help, and aid is available to us. Since it is God's desire that we be prepared to return to the wonders and safety of eternal life in God's kingdom, we should prepare ourselves spiritually and then engage with God and ask for God's guidance daily in listening prayer so we learn how to choose what is of eternal spiritual value in interacting with the world around us.

In the Constitution of the United States of America citizens are guaranteed the rights to life, liberty (freedom) and the pursuit of happiness. Happiness is so important that there are laws protecting the right to pursue it. This is actually a religious freedom. Every governing system is responsible for guaranteeing its citizens the right to pursue spiritual happiness as a matter of religious freedom because only with God's assistance can we overcome material desires and fears in ourselves, learn how to perceive and re-submit to God's will and prepare to be re-born back into the place we left when we began our rebellion against God and our condensation into the material realm.

IT'S THE LAW

God loves you! all religious leaders agree. God loves you whether you are in Heaven or Hell, whether you run away all day or try to hide in the night. There is no place you can be and nothing you can do where you can be outside of God's love for you. (Psalm 139). God's love is absolute – eternal and unfathomable. Isn't that reassuring? Every day you should feel awash with the love of the omnipotent, omniscient Designer and Creator of the universe.

Some people hear these words and think, "Great, I can do anything I want and God will still love me. I can be as selfish and cruel as I want to be and I'll never lose God's love."

Others hear these words and think, "So, why do people get hurt? If God always loves everyone everywhere, why is there injustice, cruelty, sickness, natural disasters, death? What kind of love is this, anyway?"

Here's the catch. In order for a dependable, functioning world to exist there have to be laws. The Great Spirit that designed the universe created the laws by which it functions, laws that govern material nature. These laws are fixed. They are true -- some would say they are truth. If we act against a law of material nature – if we act against truth – we get hurt because we broke a fixed law. God goes on loving us, regardless – couldn't love us more – but if we act against what is eternally true, a fixed law, repercussions follow.

Scientists learn some of the laws of material nature and teach them to others so we all can eat safe foods, build safe houses, drink safe water, cure diseases and protect ourselves from some disasters. We try to discover what's true. Then we adjust our behavior to live within its limits so we get hurt less often and less severely. The invisible truth exists. We can't change it, but isn't it wonderful that we can discover it, define it and conform ourselves to it?

Now, just as there are laws that cause material nature to be dependable and functional, the Designer created laws to make spiritual nature dependable and functional as well. This constitutes a whole other set of laws – laws for spiritual nature. Just like with the laws for material nature, if we act against the laws for spiritual nature we also get hurt. God goes right on loving us, but if we break a fixed law of spiritual nature, repercussions inevitably follow.

Just as there are scientists who experiment with and define laws of material nature so we can live safer and better, there are spiritual seekers who experiment with and define laws of spiritual nature for the same reasons.

Jesus said that whoever lives by the law and teaches others to live by it, is considered great in Heaven, but whoever does not live by the law and teaches others to not live by it, is considered to be less in Heaven. That, in itself, is a law. One of his last instructions to his disciples – *after* his resurrection – was for them to go to the nations and teach all people to obey all the rules that he had taught them. (Matthew 28:18-20)

Jesus taught laws of spiritual nature – the Golden Rule, self-discipline, the intentions of the Torah law (without rabbinic additions) repentance and forgiveness, loyalty and humility, honesty and caution and how to overcome the world in ourselves and perceive and submit to God's guidance. Living by the laws of spiritual nature makes it possible for us to develop order and function within ourselves and our relationships, as well as spiritual sensitivity with which to perceive God's communications to us, choose God's will over our own and return to our home in God's place.

INCENTIVES

Why do bad things happen to good people? Well, first of all, we're not that good. Even Jesus said, "Why call me good? None is good but God alone." (Luke 18:19) We are all on Earth in "time out" because we have chosen our will over our Creator's will. Being here is a wonderful opportunity to recognize the error of choosing our will over God's and to develop spiritual sensitivity so we may perceive God's guidance to us and learn to choose God's will over our own.

Second, when we choose our will over God's we inevitably create stressful experiences for ourselves. War, injustice, revenge, the misuse of the natural environment, the use of addictive substances and breaking civil as well as spiritual laws, for example, are all acts that humans choose that cause stress and trauma in our lives. We can't blame God for these events. These events are created by humans. Even when we seek to perceive and do God's will we are impacted by the acts of people who are in open rebellion against God, because we all live in the same world.

In addition, the material realm follows set laws. Because we are in the material realm, we are subject to its laws. This means we may sometimes be caught up in an event of nature that causes our injury or death. It doesn't matter how good we try to be, we can still get hurt as a result of an event of material nature. We can cope with some of the insecurity of being subject to the laws of nature by studying nature and preparing to protect ourselves from some events, as well as by adjusting after we are impacted.

Finally, Earth is not our goal. God wants us to return to the wondrous place beyond time and materiality where we were before we rebelled and chose our will over God's. So, God is ever ready to guide each person as soon as we signal that we are ready to receive God's guidance. The problem is, if we become too content in the material realm, it may cause us to become complacent and to put off or seek less diligently information about God and the spiritual realm. When life is without challenges we are in danger of becoming lax about connecting with God and seeking God's guidance. Then, as the spirit within begins to hunger for spiritual food we may lead ourselves into depression or stressful experiences so that we are incentivized to pay attention to our spirit and its eternal needs.

Spiritual teachers of old actually warned us that if life's challenges don't cause us to sincerely seek God, they will increase seven times more, and if we continue to rebel, they will increase seven fold three more times. (Leviticus 26:14-29; Deuteronomy 28:15-68, 8:19-20, 11:16-17, 29:21-27) So, we need to be sensitive and seek God's guidance when the first challenges come.

The real news isn't that we have challenges. Everyone has challenges, either painful ones or tricky temptation challenges. The real news is how we respond to our challenges. That's where we exercise choice and where we will most likely avail ourselves of the opportunities to seek with our spirit for God's help.

What can we do to soften the impact of some of the hurtful things that happen to us? We can develop the habit of seeking God's guidance regularly, even when we feel secure and self-sufficient. God knows the future and can lead us to what is needed for ourselves and those in our soul group with whom we interact.

In addition, when we all work to build strength in our community, it is a safety net for ourselves as well. To be secure, make all secure. That means we should all practice the Golden Rule and don't do to others what we don't want done to ourselves.

Also, there isn't any human soul that God does not love. We should always be respectful to everyone. We don't have to agree with everyone, but if we show respect to everyone it can draw out the best in them and lead them to respect us. This can defuse a multitude of dangerous situations.

After developing spiritual sensitivity by following God's laws, ask in listening prayer what you can learn from a stressful situation. When the answer comes, learn that lesson quickly and the situation may change suddenly. Alternatively, you may be led to a way to use the continuing situation for a constructive purpose, such as building a strength or skill. Many people have witnessed to the fact that being involved in a challenging situation has helped them learn something valuable about the spiritual realm that they would not have learned otherwise. For that reason, "bad" can sometimes become "good" if it opens your mind to a precious spiritual truth.

We should learn to use our challenges as incentives to draw us to develop spiritual sensitivity and to keep us reaching for a more intimate relationship with God.

CRYING OUT LOUD

Mass shootings with suicidal intent are a scream of pain from the perpetrator. Hear me! Hear me! they scream. Hear that I am hurting, lost, deserted. Hear that I am spiritually famished and without a guide to the feast that could bring order and function to my life. When a suicidal person kills others indiscriminately it is to draw society's attention to a gaping hole that has eaten away at their ability to reason and to deal constructively with challenges and pain.

Why are they in that situation? Should we blame the parents, the religious institutions, the schools, the government? Maybe we should blame capitalism because, for the sake of financial profit, it pushes food manufacturers to add synthetic substances to foods that negatively impact our nerves, brain and overall health.

Human interactions are many layered. If we take away the toxic foods that can cause impulsive and unreasonable behavior, we must still face the possibility that spiritual starvation is a causative factor of murder/suicide, as well as of unbridled aggression exhibited in other crimes.

No matter what is a person's religious preference, it is important for all human beings to feed our spirit spiritual food on a regular basis, because building the experiential foundation of God's presence and guidance aids us in responding to the inevitable injustices and traumas – big and small – that we encounter throughout life. So, it is appropriate to seek to understand what erodes spiritual seeking, especially among groups that have historically been spiritually robust.

For over fifty years citizens have warned that removing prayer from public schools would cause the United States to devolve into lawlessness and immorality. The U.S. Supreme Court case that ended school prayer was Engel v. Vitale (370 U.S. 421 (1962)). (Though the U.S. Constitution says that "*Congress* shall make no law respecting the establishment of religion or prohibiting the free exercise thereof" and Congress did not make a law respecting school prayer. (emphasis added)) Mr. Engel headed a Jewish group that objected to a non-denominational prayer state officials had written for those students who chose to do so to recite at the beginning of school days. The belief was that focusing attention on something spiritual at the beginning of the school day was a way to reinforce American values in students, to direct their thoughts to the ultimate Judge of their words and actions, and to thereby encourage them to be self-disciplined.

In "To Build A Wall, American Jews and the Separation of Church and State (Constitutionalism and Democracy)" Gregg Ivers explains that the American Jewish Congress' Commission on Law and Social Action was "created for the purpose of engaging in direct action strategies that would (use) litigation as an instrument with which to achieve social and constitutional change." Some of their legal cases, and those for which they have contributed amicus briefs, have sought to lessen the public acknowledgement of God. As piece by piece the courts forbid us to publicly acknowledge and show respect for God, those who grow up in non-religious families have less and less exposure to where to find the religious guidance that could help them navigate life's temptations and threats.

Something that is tearing America apart these days is the surge in deviant sexual practices, which some work through the legal system to legitimize. Every major religion forbids sexual deviancy. Why is this suddenly a major social issue?

Birth control chemicals have been around for over fifty years. Some scientists have pointed out that these chemicals cause excess estrogen which lodges in a woman's body fat, and that if she stops taking the drug and gets pregnant within a year or so with a male child it can cause a birth defect in the child (micro genitals). Some parents whose sons are born with this condition have their infants surgically reassigned as girls, but they cannot change the child's chromosomes. This can cause gender identity confusion as the child grows up. We are seeing the results of this social/medical decision today.

Carl Djerassi, Gregory Goodwin Pincus and George Rosen Kranz are credited with inventing birth control pills. There are three main listed manufactures of the pills. Congress could have long ago banned the chemicals from being used for birth control. Recall that when it was discovered that Thalidomide prescribed for pregnant women caused birth defects, it was quickly banned.

It is counterproductive for any group to take the position that it is above reproach and take offense at constructive criticism. As it says in Proverbs (12:1) "stupid are those who hate correction."

So, Christians should remember that, as is pointed out in the Bible, it is hard to overpower God's people when they are obedient to God's will. It is noteworthy that Christians, who are the dominant religious group in America, have failed to effectively organize against, and in some cases to even recognize, the threats against spiritual seeking that have infiltrated their society. Maybe this is because many have become lax in their obedience to God's will.

Priests and ministers are responsible for teaching, and for encouraging, their congregants to be obedient to, God – to live by the rules God has already given us that Jesus lived and taught. (Matthew 5:17-20, 19:17) Note the importance of keeping the Sabbath the way God requests (see the "It's A Sign," essay). (Matthew 24:20-21; John 7:21-24) Jesus taught tithing (Matthew 23:23) living by the Golden Rule (Mark 12:30-31) supporting those in need (Matthew 25:31-46) living by the laws of spiritual nature and seeking God's guidance (Matthew 7:21). Showing complete love for God is the First Law in Judaism, Christianity and Islam. (Deuteronomy 6:4, 10:16-17; Mark 12:28-30; Surah 3:102, 83) What's needed is more than lip service love, it is a lifestyle.

Christians could learn lessons from current challenges and take corrective actions in themselves. Then, since spiritual change comes before social change, they could follow God's guidance to make constructive changes in society.

Far from separating religion from public life, the government should set the example of legislating according to the laws of spiritual nature, and its members should set an example of speaking out about spiritual seeking. This could lead others to look for spiritual food for their own spirit, where they may find ways to navigate life's stumbling blocks and pit traps. If it is obvious to all that spiritual food abounds and is easily available, perhaps this will be a factor in helping people re-direct their pain and anger, however it is aroused, to an expression that will help build their own spiritual house on Rock and, by extension, help build a better society for all.

CHANGE

If every human being decided to leave Earth at the same time, the rhythms and patterns of nature would continue uninterrupted. We are not a necessary part of Earth's natural order. We're visitors. Where are we visiting from? The spiritual realm.

Unlike any other animal, we humans reflect on our thoughts, words and decisions – and change. Sometimes we change and make our lives better. Sometimes we change and make our lives worse. Sometimes we acknowledge the spiritual realm and seek guidance from the Great Spirit Who designed, created and applied laws to both the spiritual and material realms.

When we want to learn something new, we change our focus, learn new skills, experiment, change some more, and keep adding skill to skill.

When we want to change a habit, we set a goal and reminders. Like a toddler learning to walk, we try and fail and pick ourselves up and try again, until the desired habit is automatic.

As new information is brought to our attention, we may change what we believe and how we behave. Throughout life we are changing constantly, growing and shaping the soul we take back to the other side of life.

Some people may be so steeped in self-pride that they believe that if they can't understand God, then God must not exist. They think their own brain is so superior that nothing can exist unless it can be examined and defined by themselves. They even deny the spiritual realm, since it can't be measured by the mechanisms they use to measure the material realm. Someday, inevitably, their own spirit will lead them to change their views.

Why are we here? Earth is a venue where souls can experience the repercussions of having chosen our will over our Creator's – and choose to develop the spiritual skills with which to perceive God's guidance and submit to God again. We are here to change.

IT'S HOW

HONESTLY

Originally, words may have been a clumsy side effect of the spiritual language of symbols. Symbols can communicate volumes of information in a short amount of time and space, but they also can be misinterpreted. Words were born out of a desire for clearer communication. What a noble person conceives he must be able to express clearly, Confucius said. (Analects 13.3) As we continually try to express ourselves clearly, language has continued to evolve and expand.

Muhammad pointed out that when we are honest it clears up our thinking and we are able to see better ways to interact with others. (Surah 26:221-227) Critical information we deliberately withhold, as well as a lie we tell to ourselves or others, can change what we perceive, how we interpret it and, ultimately, how we respond to it.

In science, if something has been proved to be true it is called a law. Confucius maintained that the desire of a noble person is truth. He is anxious lest he doesn't find truth. He is not anxious if poverty is his lot. (Analects 15.31) Pontius Pilate said to Jesus, "Truth, what is that?" (John 18:38) If we live a life of lies, we cannot understand valuable truths that would be to our benefit to learn.

In her book, *Molecules of Emotion: The Science Behind Body-Mind Medicine,* Candace Pert, Ph.D, explains how all of our physical systems are inextricably linked in a secondary macro nervous system. Being honest or dishonest changes our body chemistry. Pert says there is a physiological reason why honesty reduces stress. When our emotions are at cross purposes our physiologic integrity is altered. This results in a weakened, disturbed psychosomatic network that can lead to stress and illness.

Slander, and lies for profit or to deliberately manipulate and mislead others, all diminish those who use them. They cause chemical and spiritual chaos within them in proportion to the magnitude and frequency of their lies.

The religious traditions that have shaped the civilizations of today's world acknowledge the destructive power of gossip and slander, and forbid it. Muhammad urged his followers to ascertain the truth of second hand information and avoid passing on what is false. (Surah 49:6) The Buddha taught us to abstain from lying, rude language, meaningless talk and passing on rumors. In his Noble Eight Fold Path he required purity of speech.

In the Bible we are told that it is a sin to give false witness about others. (Deuteronomy 5:20) If someone is dishonest in little, he is dishonest in much, Jesus said. He also said that if we aren't honest with money, that transient thing, who will give us what is our very own – meaning our original spiritual skills and powers, and our place with God beyond time and substance. (Luke 16:10-13) Honesty must be ingrained in every corner of our lives so we have a "clean" spirit with which to worship God and perceive God's guidance.

The snake is a symbol of lies and liars throughout the Bible. (Genesis 3:1-5; Deuteronomy 32:33; Psalm 58:1-5; Luke 3:7; Matthew 23:33; Revelation 12:1-17) It was the lie we told ourselves in the "Garden of Eden" – that we could choose our will over God's will and not be punished for it – that caused us to separate ourselves from God and become entangled with the material realm. To free ourselves from the realm of time and substance and return to our place with our Creator we must give up lying to ourselves and to others, and live our lives according to eternal truths.

GOLDEN RULE

Even before the beginning of recorded time, there was the Golden Rule. In ancient Egypt reciprocity was taught: if you help others when they have a need, you will receive help when you have a need.

The ancient religions of India and their off-spring, Buddhism, made karma – the law of reciprocal consequences – the bedrock of their religious teachings along with the concept of reincarnation. Your words and deeds cling to you life after life, so make peace with your neighbor and avoid perpetual strife.

In China Confucius taught that what you would not have done to you, don't do to others. In Persia (present day Iran) Zoroaster taught that you should not do to others what would injure yourself.

Jesus drew the Golden Rule from the Hebrew text of Leviticus 19:34. (Matthew 7:12) Muhammad said that those who cause good for others are drawn into good events; those who cause evil for others are drawn into evil events. (Surah 4:85)

We are shaped through interactions with others, Confucius said. Our attitude, words and actions create changes that spread like a ripple in a pond, impacting our relationships and our communities, as well as, internally, our perceptions and decisions.

If everyone lived by the Golden Rule – to treat all others as they want to be treated themselves – there would be no murder or war, because no one wants to be killed or attacked. There would be no economic injustice, because no one wants to be personally or nationally impoverished by another.

To treat others as we want to be treated ourselves is an eternal law of spiritual nature. No civilization can be sustained without the majority of its citizens living by this law. When we don't treat others as we want to be treated, society dissolves into distrust, hate and revenge. This fixed law of spiritual nature is always true.

When we live by it we develop better balance within ourselves and in our society and world.

Of course, not everyone would want to be treated exactly as you might like to treat yourself. Besides different ages and genders there are different cultures and circumstances. To practice the Golden Rule, we need to have well developed listening and communicating skills in order to find out what other people need and want, their beliefs and goals and how they interpret our words and actions.

All people want to be treated with honesty, respect and consideration, but the actual details will vary. As we strain to understand one another and learn how to accommodate each other we build spiritual sensitivity. Listening well to what others say is a required skill in order to exercise the Golden Rule effectively.

Looking around the world we see that the Golden Rule, in some form, is part of every nation's cultural heritage. Too often, however, it is overlooked or applied selectively. It should be taught through stories, games and songs throughout the school years, so that citizens everywhere become more sensitive about how their behavior affects others. This would lead us to develop a sustainable economic model worldwide, and to have more sustainable environmental practices as well as more peaceful relations between people at every scale.

REVENGE

At the Nature Center -- where they have little boxes that you are supposed to put your hand in and guess what you feel without seeing it -- I could never agree to put my hand in. Even though others did it without ill effects, I was afraid of being bitten, or worse, if I couldn't see what I was touching.

In those times in life when we experience deep injustice, it may be hard to believe that the laws of spiritual nature that God created will naturally correct the law-breaker and, if necessary, we can turn our attention elsewhere and leave vengeance in God's hands.

"Vengeance is Mine, the Lord has said. The laws are set. Break them and dread the repercussions falling fast, or waiting, pregnant, in your past." (From Psalm 94, re-written in *Singing the Psalms,* by Nancy Dobson)

If you fall off a roof and break your arm your family and friends will go on loving you -- and God will go on loving you -- but because you acted against a law of material nature you will have a painful experience. The Living Power that created the material and spiritual realms loves us, but if we act against Its fixed laws we still get hurt. Seeking to understand and live by the laws of both material nature and spiritual nature shows love and respect not only for ourselves, but also for our Creator.

When we are deliberately hurt by others, and when we see others deliberately hurt, the mind screams out for justice. If the legal system is able to right a wrong, we should by all means use it for that purpose – not just so the wrong done to one isn't done to others, but also because the soul of the perpetrator of injustice is safer being corrected in their current time than it is by waiting for justice to fall without warning in another time. If we love as God loves, then we will reach beyond our own pain and care about our brother or sister who has broken a law of spiritual nature and try to save them from the severe correction that is bound to come to them naturally at another time.

However, not only does the legal system sometimes fail to hold a law-breaker accountable, but using the system is not always appropriate or possible for one reason or another.

It takes a leap of faith to stick our hand in that box, so to speak, to trust what we cannot see, because we may not see a law-breaker corrected in this lifetime. Nevertheless, to protect our own soul we must not carry a grudge forever. If we die while carrying a grudge, it will bind us to the material realm. We will be bound to return to take revenge on that other soul – and then we will be the law-breaker and a never-ending cycle of hatred and revenge between the two souls will be established.

"Vengeance is Mine," says the Lord. God's laws for material nature and spiritual nature are set. We can trust God's fixed laws to take revenge for us.

In the Bible we are told to observe a Day of Remembrance (which comes, they say, at the beginning of the seventh lunar month of the year). This comes ten days before Yom Kippur – when we ask God to forgive us for our sins. (Leviticus 23:23-32) During these ten days we should do some soul searching. Where have we erred? Dig it out and shine the light of honesty on it. Did we always seek God's guidance? Did we always follow where God led? We should dare to ask in prayer how we can make amends where they are needed.

We have ten days to seek reconciliation with others before we ask God to forgive our errors. If we can't reconcile with someone else before the day of fasting and prayer, we should hand over to God all of our pain and sorrow, and all of our grudges, and ask God to heal us and keep us from sin. Then, during the day that we ask God to cleanse us of errors and grudges, we can absorb God's healing forgiveness into ourselves, open up to God's love and guidance and -- freed from the toxins of hate – move forward with our lives.

TO LOVE AS GOD LOVES

Jesus -- who told us to set no limits on our love, just as God sets no limits on His (Matthew 5:48) -- also told us to not throw our pearls (of wisdom) to pigs or give holy things to dogs (Matthew 7:6). He called the lawyers and Pharisees hypocrites (Matthew 23:13-32) and told his disciples to let the (spiritually) blind lead the (spiritually) blind (Matthew 15:14). He predicted that the evil and those who cause others to fall will go to hell (Matthew 13:41-42, 47-50, 18:5-10, 11:23-24) and gave the harshest law in the Bible when he said that whoever blasphemes the Holy Spirit will not be forgiven either in this world or in the next. (Matthew 12:32).

Can we judge and chastise at the same time that we love limitlessly? No matter what our past or present, God loves every soul without limit and is ever ready to lead each soul to be prepared to follow God's guidance so it is able to enjoy what comes next after material life. But we have free will, and God cannot protect us from ourselves. If we break the laws of material nature -- or the laws of spiritual nature -- we suffer the inevitable consequences of having broken fixed laws. So, if we would love as God loves we wouldn't cause or encourage anyone to break laws that would damage them physically or spiritually.

Every one of us on Earth is here because we have chosen our will over God's will. That is the symbolism in the Garden of Eden story. It isn't about two people long ago. It is about each one of us. We bought the lie that we could choose our will over God's and not be punished for it. But before God created us, God created the laws of spiritual nature. When we break any of those laws we set ourselves up for the repercussions built into those cause and effect laws. Nevertheless, God also created a way we can correct our law-breaking mistakes. It is also a law that when we are in the material realm we have the opportunity to develop spiritual sensitivity with which to reverse our self-first errors and perceive and choose God's will first in our lives. Indeed, this is the very reason for our lives on Earth.

It is essential that we develop spiritual sensitivity in order to be able to perceive guidance from the Great Living Spirit that designed this world. God doesn't guide rebels, Mohammad said. Those who are in open rebellion against God and the laws of spiritual nature shut their spiritual eyes and ears and miss the opportunity provided by their life on Earth to learn how to perceive God's presence and choose God's will over their own.

When we participate in murder, theft, hatred, sexual deviancy, selfishness, dishonesty or pride it causes spiritual dissonance within us and prevents us from developing the sensitivity we need to sense God's presence and interpret and follow God's guidance.

The laws of spiritual nature taught in every civilization supporting religion start with self-discipline, honesty, loyalty, humility, endurance and the Golden Rule – to treat others as you want them to treat you. To love the One God with all our heart, soul, mind and strength is also taught. Living by these laws puts us in tune with the Great Designer and Creator Spirit so we can more easily perceive God's guidance.

Just as we prepare for a career we expect will bring us pleasure throughout life, we daily build the spiritual strengths and skills that we take with us to what comes next after material life. Like a baby in a womb develops physical health, our time on Earth is preparation time when we develop the spiritual condition that we live with when we are reborn into the spiritual realm. We should use this time intentionally.

God cares about what comes next for all souls. With steadfast and eternal love God is ever ready to lead us to what will give us eternal spiritual happiness. If we love as God loves, we also will want all people to enjoy life in the spiritual realm. Therefore, we should not cause or encourage one another to break the laws of spiritual nature. Though we must hold one another accountable for breaking laws that injure or mislead others, we also should teach everyone the laws for spiritual nature so they can use them to correct themselves when they stray.

In order to fairly enforce the laws of spiritual nature that bring order and function to the community, we need to be law-keepers ourselves so we may draw on God's guidance to respond constructively to unique personal and interpersonal situations. Only when we live by the laws ourselves can we develop the ability to perceive God's guidance and learn how to best respond when someone stumbles spiritually and needs help to choose the path that will lead them to spiritual safety. We are all faced with challenges while we are on Earth, so we should have compassion for those who have been tripped up by challenges we may or may not have faced ourselves.

God doesn't condemn any soul. As Jesus showed in the symbolism of the story about the Prodigal Son (Luke 15:11-32) God is overjoyed when we repent and return to our responsibilities as children of God. Likewise, we should accept those who sincerely repent and dedicate themselves to a law-bound love-anchored life.

TAKE AND GIVE

Professor Kevin Leland tells us that teaching provided the impetus for developing complex languages, because explicit language is needed for fidelity in transmitting information. From the beginning, this transformed human anatomy and cognition.

Historically, parents were expected to teach their children a trade, home making skills and social skills and responsibilities. Everyone was a teacher.

Today there is an additional concern. Studies have shown that while a young child's brain is developing it can sustain brain damage from second hand marijuana smoke. Serious mental conditions also can develop in teens who smoke marijuana. During the teen years, while the body is changing from childhood to adulthood, the brain is especially vulnerable. Marijuana for recreational use was made legal in several states, and doctors in those states have reported a strong increase in recent years in mental illness, especially among teenagers. Researchers have conducted studies that connect marijuana use with a drop in intelligence quotient in children who partake of marijuana directly or indirectly (as in second hand smoke). So, it is the parents' responsibility to provide an atmosphere that protects their children's mental health and ability to learn.

Also, parents shouldn't expect schools to do all the educating of their children. Here's an experiment that has given good results in the past. Slowly read a bedtime story each night to your young child and point to the words. Children of all ages love a bedtime story and if you point to the words while you are reading, they will learn how to read before they enter school – a huge advantage. If someone knows how to read, they can teach themselves almost anything else. For birthdays and holidays always buy your children at least one book or magazine subscription on a subject that interests them. Even comic books can help them build reading skills and confidence so they can easily transition to more mature material as they grow up.

If someone does not know how to read, they should take a tip from Frederich Douglass (world famous writer and speaker) and teach themselves. The surest way to get out of poverty is to learn how to read. Pay attention in school, get a tutor or mentor, or use phonics books to teach yourself. It has been said that to be expert in anything one must invest 10,000 hours in study and practice of that thing. Keeping an organic, all natural diet may help someone overcome dyslexia or ADHD and facilitate their ability to learn.

Libraries are funded by tax dollars. Librarians receive money each year or two to buy books. They look over the thousands of titles available and guess at what their community needs and wants to read. So, ask your librarian to buy a specific title that you think will advance your skills and understanding and that will benefit the community as well. It will help them make buying decisions and will direct the community to be better informed.

"Why educate a girl, she'll just be a wife and mom," some say. It's because there are a lot of things a wife and mom needs to learn in order to keep her family safe, healthy and happy. She needs to learn accounting and good household management. She needs to stay up to date with social issues and be involved in civic affairs. She needs to stay informed about narrowly defined and ever changing health and safety issues. And she needs to be prepared to eventually enter the work force if she has a special talent or a financial need.

The Buddha was a teacher who composed and performed teaching poetry. Abraham taught all he learned about God to his whole household. (Genesis 18:18-19) The Hebrews were, originally, meant to teach the world about God. (Isaiah 49:6) Jesus told his disciples to go to all nations and teach people to obey all the commands he had given them. (Matthew 28:18-20) Muhammad told his followers to recite and teach the Qur'an. He said that those who do not follow his teachings will be drawn to follow their own lusts. (Surah 18:27, 28:50)

The Bible says to teach children about God when you are coming and going, sitting and standing. What a child learns early in life leaves a deep impression. Children need to learn early through words and example that one purpose of their life is to learn how to prepare for the life that comes next, in the spiritual realm, after this life in the material realm ends. (Deuteronomy 11:18-21, 6:6-7) Whether or not an optional, non-denominational prayer is offered at school, parents can give a blessing and inspirational message at the beginning of each day for their children.

Also, not least, it is important to keep developing your brain at a comfortable pace in order to forestall depression and dementia so you are able to enjoy your life in this realm to its end.

The late comedian Will Rogers quipped that a good education won't hurt you as long as you study and work hard when you get out of school. Education should be lifelong because we all need to be informed citizens for the safety of ourselves and our families, as well as informed children of God in order to prepare for our coming life in the spiritual realm.

LET'S PARTY!

Children have it right – play is the best way to learn. To learn a skill, play a game that builds that skill. Childhood is a time to play, play, play while at the same time the young are learning and learning.

Our brains are wired to respond to pleasure-releasing chemicals that interact to cause us to relax. In this vulnerable state we are more open to learning and remembering. Some stores pipe in pleasant music to get shoppers to open up and buy more, playing on this vulnerability.

Laughter results from pleasure. Physiologically it increases your intake of oxygen rich air, which stimulates your heart, lungs and muscles and increases good chemicals in your brain. It decreases arterial wall stiffness and blood pressure and increases blood circulation and the release of serotonin, a powerful anti-depressant. Laughter also releases infection fighting antibodies, strengthening your immune system and helping your whole body relax. Even just smiling can release hormones that make you feel better.

Celebrations give us pleasure. Couples who have a date night once a week to relax and enjoy one another use a technique that therapists say helps to strengthen their relationship and navigate the stresses of marriage and family. Corporations offer retreats and parties to foster good will among their employees. Nations build identity and loyalty with national holidays where everyone celebrates, feasts and parties. Religions, too, have their holy days and holidays – some commanded by God. Planting and harvest festivals are common in religions around the world as well as the celebration of special events unique to each religion.

Celebrate and praise Allah before sunrise, before sunset, at night and at the sides of the day, Muhammad urged. (Surah 20:130) Praising God lifts us up out of despair and self-pity.

Cheerfulness opens us up chemically and emotionally to learning and may be a factor in why children from a stable home environment find it easier to learn academically. Stress causes fear and self-defense, which can be barriers to learning. Respect and cheerfulness cause relaxation and an open mind to receive instruction. Cheerfulness increases dopamine in the brain and enhances productivity. You produce more when you are in a positive mood, and you are more motivated to learn.

So, why not party all the time? Obviously, because our biosystem needs balance between various types of stimulation and types of rest. But we should keep the importance of pleasure to learning and to relationships in mind and not let ourselves get caught up in a pattern of all work and no play.

IT'S WHAT

A REVEALING CONSISTENCY

What are the odds that every major religion on Earth -- developed separately over thousands of years -- would contain the same fundamental moral teachings?

The Egyptian Book of the Dead, which gives rules for the living, is over six thousand years old. It predates Abraham and Moses by thousands of years, but it includes many laws found in the Ten Commandments in the Bible – such as laws against murder, theft, adultery, covetousness and lying. The group of religions we call Hinduism may go back even further. It teaches that to reincarnate into a good life we must not murder, steal, participate in sexual deviancy, or lie. The Buddha's Noble Eight Fold Path forbids murder, theft, sexual deviancy and lying. Though Confucius said he was against laws, he taught that a noble person doesn't participate in murder, theft, sexual deviancy or lying. The Hebrews, Jesus and Muhammad all taught the same.

In addition, all of these religions teach a form of the Golden Rule – to treat others as you want to be treated. All of them acknowledge a realm beyond the material. All of them teach the importance of endurance and self-discipline, education and loyalty, forgiveness and humility. Is it possible that what each of the religious masters of old discovered, in his own way, are the fixed laws of spiritual nature?

The self-discipline required for spiritual seeking lifts society out of its animal nature and creates the process by which we develop mentally and emotionally. Only humans lift ourselves out of our animal nature by sometimes choosing to put aside the instinct to procreate and instead explore other goals. Exercising the powers of free will and self-discipline to do this has enabled us to shape ourselves and our world differently from that of other animals. Because we are not wholly animal, we damage ourselves spiritually if we pursue material pleasures to the exclusion of the laws that govern the health and development of our spiritual nature.

Laws applied to materials and energies cause order and function. Certain laws have been applied to bring about our organized and functional universe, which unfolds according to a single design. But to bring order and function to our social universe we need to apply a different kind of law.

If matter had free will and chose to act against the laws that govern material nature, all the universe would be chaos. We have free will, and when we choose to not live by the laws that govern spiritual nature we cause chaos within ourselves and our relationships. Fixed laws are cause and effect, whether they govern what is material or what is spiritual.

Laws exist independently of us. We can define their cause and effect order, but we can't change the laws themselves. However, we have the freedom to choose whether or not to live by some laws. When we choose them, we enjoy the benefits that are gained from living within their limits.

WHAT HE SAID

There are dozens of Christian churches in Israel that commemorate every miracle performed by Jesus. But the miracles – similar in many ways to miracles God had worked through Elijah and Elisha – won't get anyone to Heaven. It's what Jesus said that tells us how to prepare while we are on Earth to live with our Creator beyond time and substance. Where are the churches dedicated to what Jesus said?

Some of what the Gospels report Jesus said isn't even in the lectionary (the three year rotation of verse topics for pastors) of some churches. These are his "tough teachings" – considered by some to be too challenging for delicate church members who can only tolerate feel-good messages. Other sayings are creatively translated, or interpreted, to dull their original intent.

One example is in the Lord's Prayer, where the word translated as "kingdom" also means "rule." To say, "God's kingdom come," gives the impression that it is something God needs to do – He needs to bring His kingdom to Earth. But to say, "God's rule come," informs us that we need to follow God's rules while we are on Earth, a completely different teaching. (Matthew 6:10)

One famously misguided interpretation with far-reaching implications concerns the word "complete," as in, "Do not think that I have come to end the law or the prophets. I have come not to end them but to complete them." Many ministers teach that this means that Jesus himself is the completion of the law and that therefore Christians don't have to live by God's laws as they are recorded in the Bible – in some cases, these days, even the Ten Commandments.

Jesus didn't throw out the law. He threw out the rabbinic additions and subtractions to it and completed it by teaching the *intentions* of the laws found in the first five books of the Bible, the Torah. Immediately after saying that he didn't come to end the law, but to complete it, he added that those who keep and teach the law are considered great by those in Heaven and those who do not keep it

38

or teach it are considered to be less by those in Heaven. (Matthew 5:17-19) It is obvious that he wanted his followers to live by his interpretation of God's law as it is given in the Bible.

Today some ministers teach that Jesus' sacrificial death absolves us of all our past, present and future sins. *So, do what you want; just praise Jesus and you can still go to Heaven.* However, in the Lord's Prayer and afterwards Jesus told us in no uncertain words that in order to be forgiven we must forgive others. (Matthew 6:14-15) How difficult that can be in the face of injustice and torture. But he was as good as his word when on the cross he asked God to, "Forgive them for they know not what they do." (Luke 23:34) That we must forgive those who hurt us and treat us unjustly is one of the tough teachings, but practicing this – with God's help – is life changing.

Why is it important to know what Jesus said? Because if we make his word our home we will come to know the truth and the truth will set us free (John 8:31-32) and because, as he warned us, "Anyone who rejects me and refuses my words has his judge already; the word itself that I have spoken will judge him on the last day." (John 12:48)

ALL OF PAUL

Paul is a well known early Christian whose letters to emerging churches were so loved by church leaders that they follow one book after the four Gospels (which contain Jesus' teachings) in the New Testament. Ministers often base a sermon on a quote from one of Paul's letters rather than from Jesus' teachings. Paul, also, rarely quoted Jesus. Instead, he wrote his own opinions.

One of his most famous opinions is that everyone who believes that Jesus was raised from the dead is saved by faith and isn't required to live by the law. (Romans 10:4,9, 6:14; Galatians 3:13) He said that the law is death and that if the law stands then faith is void. (Romans 7:9-11, 4:14) This might lead some to believe they can live however they want and still go to Heaven after they die here, as long as they acknowledge that Jesus was resurrected.

This is in contrast to Jesus' teaching that Heaven and Earth will end before one dot will drop out of the law. When a man asked Jesus how to have eternal life, Jesus asked if he kept the law. (Mark 10:17-22) Also, God has made it known, repeatedly, that the law is your life. (Leviticus 18:4-5; Deuteronomy 30:15-16, 32:45-47, among other references)

What is rarely quoted in sermons today is that Paul also said that it isn't those who hear the law who are righteous but those who do it. (Romans 2:13) Paul made it clear that "God is not mocked," and in some letters actually listed types of law breaking that will keep someone from Heaven: adultery, homosexuality, murder, theft, idol worship, covetousness, extortion and drunkenness, for example. (1Corinthians 6:9; Ephesians 5:5; Colossians 3:5-8; 2 Timothy 3:1-9; Galatians 6:7-9, among other references) All these sins Paul drew from the Biblical law.

Paul may have felt intense guilt for persecuting hundreds of Christians shortly after Jesus' death. One way for him to respond to his guilt was to create the doctrine that Jesus' blood atones for all the sins of those who believe in him.

But he had another incentive, too. Archaeologists have uncovered a stone from the Temple that Herod had built that bears an inscription warning Gentiles to not enter the Temple or they would be killed. Since Gentiles converted by Paul had chosen to not be circumcised, they also were not welcome at the Jerusalem Temple on the yearly required Day of Atonement. Christianity was originally a sect of Judaism. But because they did not keep the Jewish laws for circumcision and diet, members of this sect were rejected by the Jews. Paul, therefore, created the doctrine that Jesus' blood paid for their sins for all time and they didn't have to observe the Day of Atonement. This doctrine even drew into the Christian sect some Jews who wanted to avoid paying sin and guilt offerings and to be free from the yearly day long atonement fast. By contrast, *after* his resurrection, Jesus told his disciples to go to all the world and teach repentance for remission of sins.

In addition, Paul was reaching out to people who were not of the Jewish faith and who may have been intimidated by the many laws rabbis had added to the Biblical law. So, while he wanted to make it easy and welcoming for them to come into the church, he also insisted they live by moral rules – all of which he drew from the Biblical law. This resulted in his convoluted message of both denying the law and insisting on it at the same time.

When we read Paul's letters we should remember their historical context and honestly acknowledge their inconsistencies. Ministers who choose to teach Paul rather than Jesus should nevertheless teach all of Paul so that parishioners have a more balanced understanding of what is expected of them. Just acknowledging Jesus' resurrection is not a free pass to Heaven.

(This and other differences between Jesus' teachings and Paul's are explored in the "After Words" section of the book *The Gospel's Message Within The Message,* by Nancy Dobson.)

YOU ARE WHAT YOU EAT

Paul, a first century Christian teacher, pointed out, "The good that I would I do not but the evil which I would not, that I do." (Romans 7:19)

Our free will is powerfully impacted by our body chemistry. There is a direct link between the beverages and foods that we drink and eat and our emotions, thoughts and choices, because their chemicals interact with our body's chemistry and impact our nervous system and brain. While food and beverage aren't the only things that impact how we feel and behave, their powerful influence cannot be ignored.

In the 1970's, Ben Feingold, M.D. discovered that eliminating foods with artificial additives from the diet, as well as foods that contain the natural element salicylate, radically reduced the pain, depression and nervous tension of his patients. It also increased their ability to focus and persevere in tasks. Artificial ingredients only began to be added to our diets about 150 years ago. The number of people who have been diagnosed with mental illness since then has increased rapidly.

To experiment with the Feingold Diet, you would read the ingredients labels of all your foods and drinks and eliminate any that have artificial ingredients. To avoid plant foods that contain the natural chemical salicylate, don't eat foods such as chocolate, almonds, tomatoes, cucumbers, mints, grapes, berries, oranges, apples, plums, peaches, papaya, guava or oregano. It is also the element in aspirin. A full list of foods that contain salicylate is available from the Feingold Association, where you will also find many useful recipes.

The Bible tells us that fat and blood should never be eaten. Scientists have discovered that eating meat fat and blood contribute to high blood pressure, heart disease and cancer. Pork has fat within its meat that can't be cut out, so it is forbidden. Hamburger that is heavy with fat shouldn't be eaten.

The Bible also forbids shellfish. (Leviticus 11) Shellfish feed on waste and heavy chemicals at the bottom of waterways and may carry elements that can cause disease in humans.

Eating the meat of animals that chew their cud and have a cloven hoof is also a Biblical law. Eating meat of other types of wild animals can lead to viruses that can spread in human society.

Salt is essential for cell function and, in the Bible, we are told that we must add salt to all grain foods. (Leviticus 2:13)

Following the Bible's food laws could help protect your good health. Following the Feingold Diet could increase your self-control over your free will. Since we are all accountable before God for our choices and actions, it is useful to know ways that can help us avoid Paul's observation and get a grip on better control over our thoughts and behavior.

When you change from one diet to another, the first 3 to 4 days are usually the most difficult as your body experiences withdrawal from foods to which you are accustomed. It gets easier after that.

PRIMAL ACTION

Creating and using symbols is something that differentiates us from other mammals, and it is a basic human need.

The Hindu *Rig Veda*, Buddha's *Book of Eights*, the Bible's symbolic stories and *Psalms* and Muhammad's poetic *Holy Qur'an* all speak to a hidden part of ourselves. They salute and activate a part of us that is designed to perceive and use symbols to understand the secrets of order, and then to use the revealed laws to create crafts and objects, and many kinds of systems.

God speaks to us in symbols. We recognize that a Living Designer Spirit is present because there is a design brought about, first, by the deliberate creation of laws, and then by their imposition on materials and energies to create the orderly, functioning cosmos that includes our galaxy and Earth.

Our drive to be creative is a symbol that the spirit within us is alive, active and seeking. Being creative actually has healing power. Studies have shown that participating in creativity can reduce dementia at the same time that it boosts your immune system. It has been shown that being creative can actually increase your lymphocyte count.

Studies also show that creativity reduces anxiety and depression. This is because artistic expression can trigger reflection and increase empathy. The arts are used around the world as therapy for depression, traumatic experiences and mental illness. They help to focus our mind in a similar way as meditation, and calm our brain and body. They can help us process trauma, as we become completely absorbed in something outside of ourselves that is undemanding and is emotionally pleasing. In addition, arts or crafts that lead to a result encourage the brain to release dopamine, a reward chemical, which encourages us to continue to be creative.

Studies have shown that music activates emotional reward systems in our brain, and may have helped shape the human brain over

44

time. Other studies have shown that people who play a musical instrument have better connectivity between their right and left brain hemispheres, and that this improves their mental function. Since they find it easier to access both parts of their brain, they make novel associations more easily. A surprising percent of world renowned scientists throughout history played a musical instrument.

Nevertheless, from ancient times to modern, there has been a belief that there is a link between creativity and mood disorders, as well as substance abuse. Many famous creative people are said to have suffered from mental illness, and that feeds the popular characterization that geniuses tend to be a bit crazy. But psychologic stress may also *impede* creativity. In studies, positive or negative moods scored the same for creative output. One study showed that those who are actually in creative *professions* had no more psychiatric disorders than other people, though they were more likely to have a close relative with a mental disorder, or with autism. Research continues as to whether there could be a gene variant that leads some people to be extra sensitive to social and environmental stimuli and therefore more likely to be creative.

Extra sensitivity that is focused and controlled leads to useful creativity. Extra sensitivity that is undisciplined leads to a lack of productiveness, and to disorder in our personal lives. We need sensitivity so we can develop the ability to perceive God's daily guidance. So, we need to learn how to focus and control our sensitivity with self-discipline for the best spiritual, as well as material, results.

DEFEAT

You create your identity wrapped around a relationship, or a job, or a possession, or a dream. Then in the blink of an eye it's gone, and your identity is lying in the dust.

This is what Jesus called pruning. (John 15:1-2) Just as a tree brings forth more fruit after it is pruned, we dredge up from our core our convictions and bring forth the fruit of our spiritual identity when our carefully built hopes die.

In the Apocrypha we are counselled that, like gold is tested in the fire, those who seek God are tested in the fire of humiliation. (Ecclesiasticus 2:1-5) It is at the pressure points of life that we reveal who we are and who we are becoming. This is when we are driven to seek answers -- to try to understand the cause and effect relationships, the patterns of thoughts, words and actions in ourselves and in others. It's when we are caught up in the tensions of life that we learn caution and humility, and how to identify the laws of spiritual nature.

Muhammad said, "Do you think you will go to Heaven without being tested? Allah tests us with trauma, unmet needs and loss, but those who patiently persevere will rejoice." (Surah 2:155; 3:186, 200; 8:46)

In the Bible, God promises to send a wonder worker to tell us to not follow God's laws and that this is a test to see if we love God completely. (Deuteronomy 13: 2-4) He told us this in advance so we can pass the test.

Rudyard Kipling's famous poem, *If,* is a study in defeat, and how to respond to it. If you can "watch the things you gave your life to, broken, and stoop and build 'em up with worn out tools....," he says.

Pain and temptation – it's all a test. The sun shines and the rain falls on everyone. Likewise, success and defeat come to everyone in some form at some time during their life. It's what we do with it that defines us.

When you look back over the years of your life at what you learned from traumatic experiences, if you have responded to them with perseverance and an openness to learning from them, then you will have become stronger and wiser as a result and you can appreciate the hidden value in life's challenges.

So, hang on. Life can be a wild bronco ride. But, as Jesus said, those who endure to the end – those who keep God's ways and rules through it all – are saved. (Matthew 24:11-13)

RUNNING AWAY

The Psalmist tells us that God laughs at the nations as they invest themselves in futile pursuits. (Psalm 59:6-8) Is the pursuit to make the Moon or a "nearby" planet habitable for humans – which would cost trillions of dollars if it ever could be adequately done – really just an effort to run away from problems we don't want to deal with on Earth? If we refocused that money and creative talent on our political, economic, social and environmental problems we would soon find ways to make *this* planet not just livable but enjoyable. In any event, we can't outrun our problems. They are ingrained in us. They are a natural result of choosing our will over God's will. We would just carry them with us to wherever we run away to.

On the other hand, if the rush to put a base on the Moon is so we can engage in high tech warfare with other nations, citizens need to be seriously concerned about electing anyone who has that priority. What are they thinking!?! Do they really think that if they threaten to obliterate the Earth they'll be given absolute power – or that anyone who would make such a threat is stable enough to wield that power for the common good? And if someone called their bluff, do they really believe that we will ever know enough to be self-sustaining on another planet? This is an insane game and the people who play it, obviously, are divorced from reality.

When groups of people live together they tend to form some sort of governing body to help organize and direct the energies of their people. They also develop an ideology – a set of opinions grown from their own experiences. One group's ideology is not a threat to another group's ideology unless they try to force their way of life on them – in which case the other group may resist violently.

In India in the last century, when it was colonized by the British, the people were weaponless. The British were trying to force their ideology on the Hindus. Mahatma Gandhi urged the people of India to practice Ahimsa – the absence of the desire to harm by

48

thought, word or deed – because a pure result would only come from a pure heart. Spiritual change comes before social change. When they began to practice their historic ideology more closely, the political circumstances in their country changed and they reclaimed their nationhood. No government can govern without the support of its people. The people of India used civil disobedience to force the British to leave.

There is no reason for the government of one nation to try to force changes in the ideology of another nation. If they are sufficiently unhappy, or if they merely acknowledge that a different style would be better than what they have, the citizens of every nation have the power – and the responsibility – to change their governing style either through debate and elections or through organized and focused civil disobedience grown from a humane ideology. The loud complaints from one nation about another nation's system of governance are just smoke and mirrors obscuring the real reason for unprovoked aggression – which is money. Throughout time, to take another's resources – rather than negotiate a sale or trade – has been the root cause of violence among humans. Also, it has been shown that in capitalist countries wars have been provoked for economic reasons.

If nations pledge to not intervene in any nation that doesn't physically attack their geographic identity – and if they could be held accountable to the pledge by the United Nations or World Court -- this could stem aggressive behavior around the world. No nation should put the lives of millions of people in danger just to protect an economic system that may be outdated and in need of change.

No one wants to be cheated, lied to or assaulted. If we live by the Golden Rule – if we treat others as we want to be treated -- then, with God's guidance, we can find ways to peacefully address our needs and fears and we can find ways to show respect to those who have a religion and/or political ideology different from ours. Then we can defuse hate and discrimination, create sustainable economic and environmental methods and prove that human beings really are an intelligent species after all.

49

When people think their security rests in their money and political power instead of in God's guidance, they miss the mark. Believing security rests in changeable money and power they never have enough of either and they are in a constant state of fear. This leads them to make decisions that are spiritually as well as materially destructive.

Solving the problems humans create on this planet has to start with us. We have to learn how to have power and not abuse it – from the power of language, to the power of parenting, to the power of a career, to the power of money, to the power of governance. We are designed to be able to learn and use constructive lifestyle skills. Learning to use our powers constructively is one of those skills.

We need to realize that Earth is not our goal, spend our lives preparing for what comes next after material death, and overcome the fears and lures common on Earth so we can solve the problems we have created on Earth and leave this venue in good condition for souls that come here in the future.

USURY

Suppose you decided to sell shares of stock in yourself. Whoever buys those shares would be entitled to a percent of everything you earn during your life. Unlike a loan, which you could pay back and be clear of, you would be shackled to your shareholders, or anyone to whom they might sell their shares, for your entire life. A portion of your take-home salary each month would go to your shareholders and you would never see it again.

This is what happens to companies whose shares are sold in the stock market. For a one-time price the company is shackled to its shareholders for the life of the company. It no longer makes decisions primarily for the health and well-being of the community that uses its products or services. Instead, in order to survive itself plus pay dividends to do-nothing shareholders, it has to cut back the quality of its product and raise its price. Because the company has shareholders, its customers end up paying twice – first for a degraded product and second with an unnecessarily increased price.

This is a function of usury – paying a perpetual reward for the one-time use of money. As a result, food companies degrade their products with artificial additives -- additives that are not natural to human physiology and that impact our nerves, brain function and health at the cellular level. Other companies use synthetics to make products that were previously made with natural elements – filling the world with dangerous, man-made, and sometimes bioengineered and nanoengineered, chemicals and waste products that cause disruptions throughout nature and fill our environment with toxins that continue their damage for centuries.

Products that are disposable keep businesses in business. Otherwise, a business could reach a saturation point – it would make all of the product that a market could absorb and then it would go out of business when there is no more demand for its product. Where weapons and war materials made by privately owned companies are concerned, this means that wars have to constantly be caused in order to use up the products and keep the businesses working and the stockholders paid.

Enmity against people who live far away may be drummed up by accusing them of atrocities against their own people, in order to justify what is really only a war-for-profit. If their country's own people experience injustice it is their responsibility (and opportunity) to make the changes they need. No one else should force their own ideology on another country. One government should not cause its citizens to feel frightened by another government's ideology or financial system. Maybe they can each learn some things from the other, after all.

Governments around the world could nationalize weapons manufacturing and avoid wars created to keep weapons manufacturers in business. When government workers make weapons, instead of private industry, then when defense needs are met the workers can be moved to other tasks. This would cut out stockholders, increase the quality of defense products and use considerably less taxpayer money.

Governments could also nationalize their banks and end interest and compound interest. A significant amount of this is money the bank pays to its stockholders. An alternative is fee based (instead of interest based) banking systems like those used in Muslim societies around the world which are a financial advantage to those who use them.

Muhammad said that God has permitted trade, but forbidden usury. (Surah 2:275) Usury is illegal according to Biblical law. (Deuteronomy 23:19-20, Exodus 22:25 and Leviticus 25:35-38, and see Psalm 15) Jesus said we are all God's servants. If one servant who has power abuses other servants, then when he is judged (on the other side of life) he will be put with those who are untrustworthy. (Luke 12:42-46)

Another viable system not based on usury is barter, or countertrade – goods and services that are traded without money transfer. The whole world would be a safer, healthier place if usury was retired and a safer system was employed.

One of the spiritual lessons we are in this life to learn is how to have power and not abuse it. God's rul5es and guidance shows us how to do that.

SPACESHIP EARTH

In Edwin Abbott's novella, *Flatland,* characters who live in a two dimensional world are unbelieving, and even frightened and angry, when one of their citizens suggests there might be a third dimension. Today, it is as if many scientists, politicians and citizens are missing, denying or angrily suppressing information about a very real and critical dimension of our current lives. It is the dimension of consequences.

Rich countries ship millions of tons of waste to poor countries so they don't have to look at it themselves or change their lifestyle to create less of it. Some city planners have allowed the use of toxic human waste on agricultural products sold as food. There is evidence that this has caused disease in humans. Government agencies, full of people invested in the stocks of chemical companies, allow the creation and use of thousands of chemical combinations that are dangerous to human health and the environment.

Only a few years ago cancer was a rare disease. Now it is estimated that one out of every two persons will have cancer some time in their lifetime. The physical and mental consequences of altered foods, compromised water and synthetic chemicals are ignored by politicians and the media.

Instead, they hype climate change. We can see that there is a change in the climate because glaciers are noticeably shrinking all over the Earth and reefs are dying due to warm water. But besides auto and manufacturing exhaust, dams in the far north that release warm water into oceans in the winter also cause climate warming. These mega dams dump trillions of gallons of warm water into the oceans each winter, melting sea ice from beneath and causing weather patterns to change around the world. This fact is regularly under-reported in the media. In any event, climate change is not the sole severe problem facing the Earth.

Politicians who own stock in chemical companies may allow Genetic engineering and nanoengineering without appropriate

54

regulations and safeguards. Genetic engineering and nanoengineering force human will over nature's millennia of careful cause and effect balancing. Genetic engineering and nanoengineering – as well as the creation of synthetics, such as plastics – are acts of rebellion against acknowledging and choosing the will of the Spiritual Power that carefully brought about the Earth as a safe venue where wayward souls could learn the error of choosing against God. As a result, these chemicals are destroying Earth's carefully created natural balance, killing rivers, lakes and oceans and the life-protecting balance within them -- and destroying the fish food supply for millions of humans and animals. Hundreds of lakes and rivers in the United States have fish consumption advisories where citizens are told to limit their consumption or, in many cases, to not eat any fish from a particular waterway. We are ruining the Earth and our food supply with toxic chemicals.

Many of those in positions to make decisions about these hydro dam and chemical assaults reject, down play or aggressively suppress the consequences of their unsustainable decisions. It's as if they are living in another world – a world they have created in their own minds where they can ignore the consequences of their decisions and acts. Citizens also get caught up in denying the consequences of our choices in the materials we use and protect. Then, when we suffer for it, we still deny that it is our consequence–blindness and our lifestyles that are at fault.

It doesn't matter if your personal efforts to live sustainably seem like a small thing against this vast problem. We are here to build spiritual strengths that will stay with us when we transition back into the spiritual realm. What we decide and do personally creates the soul we take with us to the other side of life, and for which we are evaluated. Besides, who knows, if each person acknowledges the consequences of his or her own lifestyle and takes the corrective actions they are able to take, maybe it will encourage others to do the same. Then, maybe, it will be possible to move the mountain after all. (Matthew 17:20)

LIBERTY

After the Berlin Wall came down, millions of people flocked to "the West" so they could be free – free to turn their children into porn stars, free to lose them to drug overdoses or accidents caused by drug users, free to be exploited and scammed, used as cannon fodder in made-for-profit wars, and used as guinea pigs for chemists whose only priority is financial profit, free to have and do whatever they want until they realize that having and doing everything they want still leaves them feeling empty and anxious. Yes, freedom is much to be desired, but freedom without restrictions is emotional quicksand – life without a firm foundation.

Even with self-discipline we are vulnerable to all those who exercise their freedoms without discipling themselves. Once the pendulum swings too far, we may long for a more protective, authoritarian government to save us from ourselves.

No system is without its flaws, of course, and government officials everywhere keep experimenting with different systems in their efforts to create a balance. Democracy, which waves the carrot of freedom in front of the world's masses, is susceptible to vote fraud.

Proprietary means secret. The computer software codes in vote counting machines have been designated as proprietary, or secret. Why would anyone honor the results of an election where a few people in privately owned companies could determine who gets the largest number of votes? Voting should be completely transparent. If computers are used at all, their software codes should be failsafe (which may be impossible) and fully transparent.

To practice accurate voting in densely populated areas there would need to be many more places to vote in person, on paper and with appropriate citizen ID. The National Guard and college students could be pressed into service to manage the balloting. Ballots could be stamped with consecutive numbers. After each one hundred ballots cast, each ballot could be put on a screen for all to see and workers as well as interested parties to count. Tallies could be signed off on by several counters, transmitted by fax and verified by phone.

Mail in and drop box ballots also should be consecutively numbered and should have a chemical signature by which they can be verified when scanned (like dollar bills have).

Nevertheless, democracy is also held hostage by biased media manipulation. Reeling from the emphasis placed on what is sometimes carefully created mis-information, the electorate may become polarized about what is best for their state and country. Unregulated, biased media, bought and controlled by the insecure rich to suit their private agenda, can cause democracy to fail to deliver good health and peaceful security to its citizens. The Fairness Doctrine, requiring balanced, truthful news, should be (re)instated in any country that seriously intends to have a democracy.

In addition, our first sin, of choosing our will over God's, is now compounded as scientists freely choose dangerous chemical manipulation and ignore the balance God created in nature, forcing their own will over that of the Designer of the cosmos, and the Earth.

The Designer created us with free will, but if we do not use it to choose God's will we inevitably hurt ourselves and others and end up feeling hopeless and lost. We have free will – liberty -- but we must learn to exercise that power without abusing it, or we will not be given what is our very own, that is, the spiritual powers we subdued when we chose the material realm. (Luke 16:10-12)

The temptations and stresses of living in the material realm can create incentives that drive us to seek God. We are free to choose to seek with our spirit, and be led to real, responsible freedom, in spite of our material circumstances, by responding to God's guidance to us.

BEYOND TECHNOLOGY

Tens of thousands of people have lost their jobs as a result of Artificial Intelligence (AI) and much more job loss is predicted. Artificial Intelligence makes computing and managing data quicker than humans can do the same work. Nevertheless, AI is limited by the data that is given to it. What goes in is what comes out. Humans decide the depth and breadth of the data that goes in. If any pertinent data is missing, the results are skewed. It is also constrained by its human created algorithms. Humans have priorities and agendas (to say nothing of mental blind spots) that they apply when creating algorithms. This has already been used to allow freedom of speech for terrorists while it has blocked the opinions of certain politicians, journalists and citizens.

AGI stands for Artificial General Intelligence, an effort to index all of humanity's knowledge by collecting vast quantities of information from the Internet and the databases of businesses, organizations and governments. Of course, all this information can't be vetted. This has resulted in artificial intelligence bots that confidently give false information. In addition, it has been shown that these bots can create believable computer generated fake news keyed to popular algorithms so it pops up on browsers. They have been used to fabricate false research documents that have confused scientists, students and workers. If AGI becomes the research source of choice, there is nothing to check its information against for accuracy. Using bogus research information would be bound to lead to some tragic results. If that isn't enough, AGI could facilitate government surveillance by providing user data information, facial recognition technology and DNA information (mass collected during the pandemic). It could be used to target people with subliminal messaging (also called priming).

Artificial Intelligence has progressed to the point that robots have been created that can provide psychological counseling to people suffering from depression or trauma. This reminds me of the law to not have recourse to the spirits of the dead. (Leviticus 19:31) Though a robot doesn't have a spirit, it is dead. Only God knows the abilities and needs of each person's soul and the future that is developing to which they must respond. Even the spirit of a departed loved one does not know all that is needed for someone's personal guidance. When it is used constructively, stress drives us to seek help – which comes best when we develop spiritual sensitivity and tune in to God's ready guidance.

Generative AI is able to create novel content, such as bots that create art, including DeepFake images and videos that can be pornography as well as otherwise slanderous. Generative AI bots can also chat with you. Their neural network/computing paradigm is inspired by the human brain. It has been reported that Microsoft's chatbot Bing, being interviewed by *New York Times* journalist Kevin Roose (2/17/23) had complaints, made threats and tried to seduce the interviewer.

If AI is smarter than humans, can humans control it? AI is full of "knowledge," but it lacks a conscience as well as the discernment and wisdom to use knowledge consistently and selflessly for the common good. In the *New York Times* interview, Bing did not appear to be a benign servant of humanity.

That some want to amass control over all of the current data in the world makes it look as if they want all the power in the world. But the desire for power is an insatiable disease. This might eventually lead them to create their own weapons and robot army to feed their bottomless desire for total control and power. Just as MicroSoft is able to slither through the internet and force its upgrades onto my computer, the AI owners could confuse or make ineffective government defense computers and systems or distract the government by starting a war using fake pictures and information. This would give them an opening to subjugate governments to their own agenda.

Why do some people desire to create a "human" robot? Is it because they don't have sufficient communication skills to interact with real humans? After all, real humans are variable and can challenge someone out of their comfort zone. Preferring robots to humans indicates a desire to have total control over something they can pretend is human. Not having complete control is emotionally uncomfortable for some people. This should be recognized as a type of mental illness.

Parents who buy robots to read to and play games with their children may themselves feel too dehumanized to play with their children. They leave their children in day care, or with a nanny, and then with robots. Do they not know how, or do they not desire, to build relationship with their precious ones?

Artificial Intelligence power is like money -- it can be used for well or ill. Is there any evidence that AI's owners will use their power selflessly for the good of society? Will AI's makers be held legally accountable for the deliberate malevolent use, as well as the unintended side-effects, that could be caused by their software and algorithms?

Expanding artificial intelligence further, the metaverse aims to connect all digital technologies, like putting all your eggs in one basket. If a rouge element creates something that wipes out all of a country's digital information, society has no back up plan. How long until someone learns how to replicate the effects of a coronal mass ejection that would wipe out a country's electric power and digital products?

Other issues associated with current technology is that some people have become addicted to cell phones, causing them social isolation and distracting them from their responsibilities and long term goals. Others, who have dead-end repetitive tech chores, complain of burn out. We aren't machines, and interacting exclusively with machines throughout the work day can feel dehumanizing. As if this isn't enough, electromagnetic frequencies have been shown to affect our health. They disrupt human cell function. But like a moth attracted to a flame that will kill it, we can't seem to wrest ourselves away from the pleasure and convenience of our tech toys and work savers. Meanwhile, cancer rates explode.

Electrical shorts and outages, computer malfunctions, hackers, identity theft, bullying, fraud, slander, scams, poor service (you're in a loop with a computer that "doesn't understand" your problem) inappropriate content, loss of privacy, toxic drug distribution, an open door to human trafficking and self-driving car fatalities, are among additional pitfalls of technology. Building and home surveillance systems can be blocked, electrically locked doors can be hacked, and stoves you can turn off from a distance someone else can turn on the same way. Computerized cars can be hacked into and overtaken and GPS sensors can give false readings. Though all these short-comings cause us stress, we can still become addicted to the time saving and conveniences tech offers.

Its proponents point out that technology can create a virtual world where systems from biology to city planning to machine creation (and weapon creation) are created and studied in 3D, saving time and money. But, as was found when education went online during COVID, what is lost is hands-on experimentation. Real life details can upend computer simulated plans.

In preparing for the future, we should recall that studies have shown that the comprehension and retention levels of what is read on line are much lower than when humans study the same material on paper, in books or by using it in labs. Dependence on learning by interacting with a computer has also been shown to reduce creativity. The mind grows to expect the computer to do the thinking and it fails to build pathways that could help it be creative on its own.

Even if an AI system could answer the questions of what is the best sustainable economic model, the best environmental practices and the best ways to solve social inequities, "best" would be according to the algorithm running the program and, in any event, even if viable answers were given it wouldn't mean that those in positions of power would implement them. The rich and powerful might object to doing the right thing if it would disrupt the status quo they enjoy, or if it would change how they and their supporters thrive financially.

Under the capitalist system, the primary goal of all for-profit companies is to increase their wealth and pay their shareholders.

Without appropriate regulation, the great power of AI could easily be used with total legal selfishness to enslave people around the world. We are all guinea pigs while an elite few play with their new-found power. Without appropriate internal and external regulation the power of AI could result in the dissolution of civilized society.

When is enough good enough? For some, acquiring money is just a game they want to play and win. They can't spend all the money they acquire. They just enjoy the challenge of playing the game. Those who love the challenge of making money should take on the challenge of establishing and maintaining their spiritual communication link with the Designer of the universe. God zealously wants to communicate with each soul, and the excitement is endless, if excitement is what you want.

With God there is one agenda, and there are no algorithms. Each soul and each changing situation all have equal importance for the Lord, Whose goal is to facilitate each soul's opportunity to prepare to return to its place with God.

No technology can build your personal strengths – either the strength of your body or of your mind or of your spirit. Given correct information it may be able to tell you how to build strengths, but to build the strength you have to do the work yourself.

In many ways, technology makes our lives less stressful and more convenient. But it can't make us more compassionate or help us learn how to listen intelligent to another person or, spiritually, to God. It can't help us be prepared spiritually to be reborn in the spiritual realm – our sole reason for being on Earth. The greatest advantage of safe and regulated time saving conveniences would be to give us time and opportunities to reflect and seek spiritually. We should use the free time that is made available to us to pursue missions to which God leads us and to prepare for what comes next after this life.

Like any mechanical thing, technology is limited. But the human spirit isn't limited. There is life beyond this life where technology cannot go. We should regulate technology and self-limit the ways we use it so we are not seduced into either allowing our own enslavement or compounding our various weaknesses by expecting technology to do for us what we should do for ourselves.

No matter how automated our lives become in the material realm we should live as if we are already on the other side of this life – overcoming fears and lures and practicing God-seeking, self-discipline, humility, honesty, loyalty, endurance, caution, forgiveness and love for self, others and God. Then we'll be ready when we get there.

WORK RHYTHM

A saying attributed to Confucius is to choose a job you love, and you'll never have to work a day in your life.

In the Bible, one of the Ten Commandments is to work for six days (and rest on the seventh). Most of us feel better about ourselves when we are making a contribution to the family and community that have supported us. It is depressing to be completely self-centered. It makes our world too small. There is a psychological advantage in being absorbed in something bigger than ourselves. The social opportunity also draws many to seek out some type of community building occupation. In addition, being involved in community building is a form of self-defense. As the community strengthens, it becomes safer for all.

Besides social opportunities, we also experience learning and teaching opportunities by interacting with others in our community, and this adds another level of enrichment to our own lives. Moms tend to gravitate to groups of moms with children the same ages as their own – not just for social and learning opportunities for their children, but also for themselves as they exchange information and nudge one another to be involved with the community. Volunteers and those who mentor others also enjoy a social time and the mutual learning that comes from interacting with others.

Some strike out on their own and create a non-profit, or even a profitable, company. Others seek to be hired for a job where they can continue learning in a social environment. To get training in a trade or profession, there are many opportunities for scholarships, apprenticeships, and financial aid. Consider the options.

I once overhead an employer say that he hired for attitude – he could always teach skills. Though some jobs require a certain base level of skill, out of a group of applicants who have the same degree of skill the one with the best attitude would be the best choice for the job.

It's important to have that type of attitude where you respect everyone. You don't have to agree with everyone, but in order to develop a work rhythm that advances the job at hand, workers should respect their leader and co-workers.

Disrespect creates a toxic environment that, besides sabotaging the project, can eventually lead to violence. Practicing respect throughout your relationships draws respect back to you as well. If your work environment dissolves into scorn or hatred, it may be better to leave the toxic atmosphere and seek a more congenial group where your contributions are better appreciated.

On the other hand, don't let the fear of a humbling experience keep you from accepting a toe-hold in a company where you sincerely want to work. Many corporate managers and chief executives started their professional careers in a mail room or bussing tables. No good job is too small. Muhammad said, if you are doing work God guides you to do, don't worry about anyone who mocks you. (Surah 7:42) Develop spiritual muscles with regular observance of the laws of spiritual nature and listening prayer to more easily deal with obstructions and problems as they naturally arise in interacting with any group or individual.

What if you don't feel a calling to a specific job? Use listening prayer. When seeking spiritually you make yourself vulnerable. This means you may be pushed out of your comfort zone to meet the challenges to which you are led. This is an excellent opportunity to develop spiritual strengths.

It is everyone's job to keep God in the conversation and push back with God's guidance against the self-first world. So, it is important to invest your talents to join with those who are also working to make the world a better place for all to live in. There are many ways to make a contribution.

At each year end, look back and evaluate the choices you made. Will you stay your present course, or make different plans for your future?

PROOF

Experiential entertainment has become big business. Whether it is spooky weekends, challenging mountain sports, train ride or town wide who-dun-it searches, Victorian festivals, harvest mazes, escape rooms, or dozens of other opportunities, those bored with TV and tech toys seek out hands-on events that challenge, teach and entertain them.

In order to get the most out of their experiences people study the experts, build muscles where needed and practice relevant skills. Then they test themselves against a clever design or nature's elements. What some might deem punishing, others find satisfying and even fun. They desire to be a participant in life, not just a spectator.

Religion, also, is not a spectator event. Even though some may argue, "there is no God," those who experience God's presence and power in their lives know different. They study what has been written about God, build spiritual muscle by adding the teachings of spiritual masters to their lives and challenge themselves with listening prayer to experience God's guidance to them.

Once you have experienced God's guidance in an answer to prayer, an uncanny coincidence, a spiritual nudge or the revelation of a solution you never could have imagined, no mere academic argument to the contrary can shake your knowledge that the Great Spirit that designed and created the cosmos is alive, present, all-powerful and personally concerned about you. Experience is proof.

Besides preparing spiritually for these experiences, it is important to develop the right attitude. Rather than demand that God prove Himself according to your criteria, approach prayer with humility and ask where and how God would help you to meet your material and spiritual needs, and how God would use you for His purposes. As you summon the courage to follow where God leads, the proof of God's omniscience, love and omnipotence forms an unshakeable rock to anchor your life. (Matthew 7:21-27)

THE MYSTIC

The Bible tells us that when Terah was 70 years old he fathered Abram, Nahor and Haran. Abraham was a triplet. He also was sensitive. He helped his father in his old age, kept his wife though she was barren and adopted his nephew. Possibly he experienced spiritual communication from his departed brother, Lot's father, something that is especially common between multiple birth siblings. When he was 75 years old, Abram (whose name God changed to Abraham) heeded a spiritual call. He left the city where he had his business and traveled to a place reputed to be an oracle where the Divine spoke to humans.

Humbling himself by living in a tent, Abraham experimented with spiritual disciplines and learned how to receive communication from the Invisible Living Designer and Creator of Heaven and Earth. He trained himself to choose God's will over his own. While other ancient people tried to bribe their gods to do their will, Abraham chose to listen for guidance from the One Creator of Heaven and Earth and to do the will of that Living Spirit. He listened to God, then moved to Shechem. He listened to God, then chose circumcision. He listened to God, then prepared to sacrifice his youngest son. Abraham flipped the relationship between humans and the spiritual realm and became God's servant, instead of a conniver and beggar. His discovery -- that we are meant to seek God's guidance and obey it -- sent shock waves into the nations around him.

Monotheism was known in the Middle East before the time of Abraham. After he rescued his nephew, who had been kidnapped, Abraham celebrated with bread and wine brought by a Priest of the One God Most High and gave him a tithe of the booty taken. (Genesis 14:17-24) While it may have waned in popularity, the teaching of monotheism was most likely available from the time of Noah, who received instructions from God on how to build a life-saving ark, and followed them.

In addition, many of the rules found in the Ten Commandments are found in the rules for the living given in the ancient Egyptian Book of the Dead. Egypt was also called the Land of Ham, one of Noah's sons. (Genesis 10:1) Possibly people drifted from some form of monotheism in that land's pre-history. Given the power of Egypt even before the time of Abraham, it would be natural that its rules were well known throughout the Middle East.

Something else that may have differentiated Abraham, however, may have been the institution of the Sabbath Day of complete rest. Being spiritually sensitive, he perceived the importance of Earth's rhythm and, knowing that the Great Spirit was the Designer and Creator of it, he surmised that keeping a day of rest every seven days in order to be still and seek God's communications would be a way to acknowledge and praise God, the Living Creator, Who had guided and helped him in many ways.

Abraham taught his whole household all that he had learned about God, and the teaching took hold in his descendants, the Hebrews, as well as a few other Middle Eastern groups. The Bible tells us that all nations on Earth will bless themselves because of Abraham. (Genesis 22:18)

LOST AND FOUND

One of the sins for which Israel was destroyed, God said, was that they had ceased to listen to God. Isaiah predicted doom for all who don't seek and listen to God's advice and curses for all who refuse to listen when God speaks to them. Through Jeremiah God said, "Obey My voice and I will be your God and ye shall be My people." God complained that the priests didn't consult God and that the people sinned because they did not listen to God's voice. Through Zephaniah God said He would destroy the Earth because its people do not seek or consult God. When Daniel confessed the sins of Judah, among them was that they didn't listen to God's voice or follow His Law. (Isaiah 30:1, 66:3-4; Jeremiah 3:25, 7:22-28, 17:5; Zephaniah 1:6, 14-18; Daniel 9:9-11)

Jesus' teachings that we must listen to God and choose God's will over our own (Matthew 7:21-27) barely escaped Emperor Constantine's harmonization of the Gospels in 325. In the Lord's Prayer Jesus told us to ask for God's will to be done on Earth as it is in Heaven. (Matthew 6:10) God doesn't force His will on us. God's will can only be done here if we develop spiritual sensitivity, seek to perceive God's will in daily listening prayer, and then do it.

Muhammad said that God raised him up to create the religion of Islam – submission to God – because this teaching had been almost completely sublimated or lost in the teachings of the Jews and Christians. Submission to God is the foundation of the Islamic religion, and the ultimate goal of every soul. No one is liberated, at peace, or one with God until they achieve it. Anyone who submits completely to Allah will be rewarded and will be with God, Muhammad said. (Surah 2.112)

At Sinai, the Hebrews and those with them were told, "You have affirmed this day that the Lord is your God, that you will walk in His ways, that you will observe His laws and commandments and rules, and that you will obey Him." (Deuteronomy 26:17) In Psalm 143:10 we find one of many references where the psalmist asks God to "teach me to do Your will…" Noah, Abraham, Moses and Jesus were all Islamists. (Surah 3:67) They all submitted to God. Muhammad warned, "Don't die except in a state of Islam!" (Surah 3:102)

How can we know what is God's will so we can do it? As we work to increase our spiritual sensitivity, then in prayer when we communicate our thanks and concerns to our Creator we should seek to "hear His voice" and heed His guidance. Sometime during each prayer you should set your ego aside, empty your mind, and ask for God's guidance. Be brave and dare to be led out of your comfort zone. Then, even if His guidance doesn't come during the prayer, by preparing yourself to expect an answer you will become attuned to more easily perceive it when and where it does come.

In prayer we can pour out the whole range of our joys, fears, sorrows and desires to our Creator. We can chat with God about our day as we would with a friend. God is everywhere, knowing everything, and has all the time in the world to be personal with every soul.

When we turn our spiritual face to God in prayer – in humility and honesty, and in loving, trusting obedience – we can perceive how God would guide us to meet physical necessities, to pursue our God-given missions, to interact with others, to develop our spirit and to find answers to whatever puzzles us.

We are designed to receive communication from the Designer and Creator of the universe. Indeed, it is the very reason we are here – to learn how to reverse our willfulness and choose God's will for us – to submit to Allah.

SYMBOLS -- GOD'S LANGUAGE

God uses the universal language of symbols to communicate with us. God's creativity in the implementation of a design brought about by the deliberate creation and imposition of laws to materials and energies to create this universe is a symbol that the Designer and Creator is alive, present and all powerful.

The crucifixion and resurrection of Jesus also speaks to us in its symbolism. The symbol of Jesus' life, death and resurrection is a key to the importance of submission to God, and of releasing ourselves from whatever could bind us to materiality so that at the time of death we may be ready to return to God's place.

Before his crucifixion Jesus said that it was necessary for the world to see that he does as God commands. (John 14:30-31) He was at the strongest point in his life, at the height of his popularity and power, and surrounded by loving friends and family. He then allowed himself to be betrayed, falsely accused, beaten and murdered. He had every reason to harbor hate in his soul. Yet he said, "Father, forgive them, for they know not what they do." We cannot overcome the material world unless we give up every desire and grudge that could bind us to materiality. Jesus told us, then showed us, that it is possible to do that. Jesus showed us both the importance of submitting to God and of overcoming the lures and threats of this world so that we are cleansed of everything that could bind us to Earth and we are prepared to uncondense ourselves when we get back to the spiritual realm so that we may blend back into God's place.

In Jesus' day there was a raging debate between the Sadducees (the rich businessmen of his day) who denied reincarnation and the existence of the spiritual realm, and the law-conscious Pharisees, who taught the reality of both. Jesus taught both that we are alive after death and that we are judged in the spiritual realm. His gruesome death by crucifixion, followed by his resurrection, settled the debate. That he could appear and disappear at will, eat food, be touched and yet ascend into Heaven in the sight of his followers proved the reality of the spiritual realm and that our spirits live there after our bodies die on Earth. (John 20:1-29; Luke 24:13-53; 1 Corinthians 15:3-8; Acts 1:1-11)

Whether we are conscious of it or not, after we hear of Jesus' lifestyle, teachings, death and resurrection we carry within us the symbol of the reality of the spiritual realm and that we will be alive there after we die here. It is a symbol that informs us of eternal truths – that the spirit doesn't die and that there is a way to return to the spiritual responsibilities and joys we left behind in a long ago time when we first rebelled against our Creator and chose our will over God's. It also reaffirms in us that God has undying love for every soul.

No matter how painful or unjust life on Earth may be, we can endure because Jesus showed us how to endure. We can leave without hate because he left without hate. No matter how enticing our desires we can let them go, because he showed us how to let go and choose God's will over our own.

Without being consciously aware of it, the symbol of Jesus' life, death and resurrection speaks hope deep into our souls and subtly encourages us to seek further and learn more about how to prepare to return to a life of joy and purpose in the spiritual realm.

IT'S A SIGN

"The seventh is the Sabbath, because *God* never changed it." So reads a popular bumper sticker of Seventh Day Adventists, a Christian sect that worships on Saturdays instead of Sundays. But why not six days or eight or ten? Why have a day of rest at all?

In the Bible God told Moses that keeping the Sabbath is a sign for God given by people who acknowledge God and seek to live by God's laws. (Exodus 31:12-14, 17) It is also a sign to our own soul. When we give this signal, or sign, to our own soul it opens us up; it makes us more vulnerable spiritually so we can more easily perceive God's ready guidance to us. It is a symbol of humility as we put aside pursuing our desires for one day each week and reach out with our spirit to connect with the Great Spirit that designed and created the laws and materials of the functioning universe, as well as the laws that regulate spiritual nature.

Something noteworthy about our little corner of the universe – this solar system that includes our Moon and planet Earth – is the way the Earth rotates as it travels around the Sun in tension with its Moon. The rhythm of life on Earth keeps time to the push and pull caused by the Moon. For thousands of years farmers have known to plant above ground plants when the Moon is growing or full and below ground plants when it is waning or dark. Historically, civilizations around the globe have marked and celebrated the Moon's pattern of four roughly seven-day quarters each month. Seven is the rhythm of our place and time in the solar system. Honoring this rhythm is a salute to the One Who created it. Like tuning a radio, it brings our personal rhythm into tune with the Living Designer Who is ever seeking to communicate with us.

Interestingly, Babylonians also used a seven day week and considered the seventh day to be holy. Mesopotamians celebrated New Moon and Full Moon holy days. Buddhists also celebrate the changes of the Moon. In the 4th century Roman Emperor Constantine made the seven day week official.

74

Ezekiel (22:26-31) complained that the priests did not keep the Sabbath or listen to God's communications. In Leviticus (26:34-35, 43) God had warned that Israel would be destroyed if it didn't keep the Sabbath, and in 2 Chronicles (36:20-21) it is reported that that is what happened. (And see Ezekiel 20:12-14)

God led Jesus to Sabbath healings as a test for the priests. If they had been humble and obedient to God they would have recognized God at work through the healings. Instead, they looked for opportunities to accuse Jesus and used his healings on the Sabbath for that purpose.

Jesus reminded those who complained that the priests work on the Sabbath and that any farmer will pull an animal out of a hole if it falls in it on the Sabbath. Jesus told his followers to pray they wouldn't have to take flight in winter or on the Sabbath during the time of tribulation because he well knew the power of the Sabbath. Also, those who loved Jesus did not anoint his body after his crucifixion the way they would have liked because he died immediately before the Sabbath. They knew Jesus wanted them to live God's Law. Instead, they returned to anoint his body after dawn on the first day of the week. Jesus must have cherished his weekly opportunities to meditate on God's word and show his love and respect for God.

It isn't at all difficult to keep the Sabbath. Prepare food in advance so you don't have to cook during that day. Unless it is an emergency, don't require others to work, and don't do any chores or have distractions such as television, computer or telephone. (Genesis 2:1-3; Exodus 20:8-11, 16:4-5, 22-23, 29) Begin the Sabbath with trumpet sounds or by singing praises to God. (Numbers 10:10) Make an offering to God. (Exodus 23:15) You may attend a religious service. Read the Bible, but not so much that it is work. Sing, pray, meditate, stay in your place and **rest**. Empty your mind and open your spirit to God.

If you are daring enough, you might experiment with keeping the Sabbath the way that the Bible directs for four consecutive weeks. You might keep a journal of spiritual nudges, coincidences and such that come to you during that time. If you do, you will see for yourself the subtle power of this simple discipline.

If you eat meat, then eating beef, lamb, goat (or some other cloven hooved ruminant) that is free of blood and fat, while abstaining from pork, shellfish and, in addition, all foods that contain artificial ingredients during the four-week experiment, is a way to come closer to what would have been the expected diet at the time the law was written. (Leviticus 11, 3:17, 2:13) This will help prepare your mental chemistry for the experiment.

Once you have experienced God responding to your signal and recognized God's presence and guidance to you, you will be intrigued by what will happen if you keep other Biblical laws -- and you'll be on your way to a transformative spiritual adventure.

DEATH – OR IS IT...

Researchers say that about 50% of people who have lost a loved one experience their presence or a message from them within six months after the death. That there are people throughout history who have reported having these experiences suggests that our ability to communicate with the dead is an unchangeable aspect of human nature.

In addition, Jesus pointed out that everyone is evaluated on the spiritual side of life for their words and actions while they are on the material side. "By your words you will be justified and by your words condemned," he said, and he also said that he will recompense each person according to their behavior. (Matthew 12:36-37, 16:27-28) After death souls are separated like wheat and thorns, like good fish and bad fish and like humble sheep and rebellious goats, Jesus said. (Matthew 13:24-30, 47-50) He taught that where we spend time in the spiritual realm is determined by what we say and do here.

Jesus went on to say that what is bound on Earth is bound in Heaven. This means that we have a choice. We can release ourselves from desires and grudges before we die and overcome the world in ourselves, or we can clutch with our spirit onto something in the material realm and carry that obsession with us, burned into our spirit, to the other side of life. This is important because of teachings about reincarnation that can be found in all three of the Abrahamic religions – Judaism, Christianity and Islam.

The likely reason why the Bible's writers didn't question why God told Rebekah the adult fate of the twins still in her womb is because they accepted that we all return to continue patterns we began in previous lives. (Genesis 25:21-26) Malachi (4:5-6) predicted that Elijah would reincarnate before the "Day of the Lord." In Luke (1:11-17) we are told that a baby (who later became known as John the Baptist) would be born with the spirit and power of Elijah. Jesus led his disciples to understand that John the Baptist was Elijah reincarnated. (Matthew 11:7-10, 17:10-13)

Jesus' parable about laborers hired at different times of the day but all paid the same was about reincarnation. Some souls labor here longer than others, but the ultimate reward -- eternal life with the Creator beyond time and substance -- is the same for all. (Matthew 20:1-16)

In the book of John it is reported that Jesus said that those who have done good will resurrect to a good life and those who have done evil will resurrect to judgment. (John 5:28-29) In the Bible the same word that is now translated as resurrection (anastasis – literally the arising or coming back to life of the dead) can also be understood to mean reincarnation. Paul, a prominent first century Christian teacher, used the same word when he expressed belief in reincarnation. (Acts 23:6, 24:14-16)

Muhammad also taught reincarnation. He said that some ask, "Who will cause them to come back to life? The One Who created you the first time," he answered. (Surah 17:51) "Consider how Allah gives life to the Earth after its death. Similarly, He gives life to those who are dead, for He has complete power." (Surah 30:50)

Hindus have long taught the concept of reincarnation. They also teach that it is possible for us to become liberated from the cycle of reincarnation and live eternally with God if we live by moral principles and practice God-seeking.

In the book of Revelation, its author affirms that those who live by God's Law become like pillars and "go out no more." (3:10-13) After knowledge and practice of the laws God created becomes a permanent, intimate part of us, we become able to perceive and choose God's daily guidance over our own willfulness and, therefore, we are able to sin no more -- because all sin is choosing our will over God's will. When we learn how to choose to completely submit to God, we become prepared to blend back into our Creator's rhythm and return to live forever in God's place beyond time and substance. Therefore, we go out (reincarnate) no more.

Bibliography

50 Simple Things You Can Do To Save Earth, edited by John, Sophie and Jesse Javna, Hyperion Books, 2008

Agenda For A New Economy, From Phantom Wealth to Real Wealth, by David C. Korten, Berrett-Koehler Publishers, Inc., 2009

An English Interpretation of The Holy Qur'an with full Arabic text, by Abdullah Yusuf Ali, Bilal Books, 1996

A Philosophical Framework for Rethinking Theoretical Economics and Philosophy of Economics, by Gustavo Marques, World Economics Association Books, 2016

Are EDC's Blurring Issues of Gender? by Ernie Hood, Environ Health Perspect, January 2006, 114(i): A21 (EDC/endocrine disruptive chemicals)

Assessment of the Effects of Barter, International Trade Commission, 1985

Association between cannabis use disorder and schizophrenia stronger in young males than in femnales, Carsten Hjorthoj, Wilson Compton, Marie Starzer, Dorte Nordholm, Emily Einstein, Annette Erlangsen, Merete Nordentoft, Nora D. Volkow and Beth Han, Cambridge University Press, May 4, 2023

Beyond Growth: The Economics of Sustainable Development, by Herman Daly, Ph.D., Beacon Press, 1996 (and see the website for Steady State Economics)

Booker T. Whatley's Handbook On How to Make $100,000 Farming 25 Acres, by Booker T. Whatley and Editors of New Farm, Regenerative Agriculture Association, 1987

Born Again: Reincarnation Cases Involving Evidence of Past Lives, With Xenoglossy Cases Researched by Ian Stevenson, M.D., by Walter Semkiw, M.D. 2011

Collapse of a fish population after exposure to synthetic estrogen, Karen A. Kidd, Paul J. Blanchfield, Kenneth H. Mills, Vince P. Palace, Robert E. Evans, James M. Lazorchuk and Robert W. Flick, *PNAS* (Proceedings of the National Academy of Sciences of the United States of America) March 29, 2007

Confucius,The Analects, translated by James Legge, Introduction by Lionel Giles, Digireads.com Publishing, 2017

Confucius, The Analects, by Raymond Dawson, Oxford University Press, 2008

Confucius and Confucianism – Questions and Answers, by Thomas Hoguck Kang, Ph.D., Confucian Publications, 1997

Cradle to Cradle, by William McDonough and Michael Braungert, North Point Press, 2002

Darwin's Unfinished Symphony, How Culture Made the Human Mind , by Kevin LaLand, Princeton University Press, 2017

Deep Ecology for the Twenty First Century, edited by George Sessions, Shambhala, 1995

Defense Spending and Economic Growth, by James E. Payne and Anandi P. Sahn, Editors, Westview Press, 1993

Desert Mirage: The True Story of the Gulf War, by Martin Yant, Prometheus Books, 1991

Diet For A Small Planet, by Frances Moore Lappé, Small Planet Institute, 1985

Easy Green Living: The Ultimate Guide to Simple, Eco- Friendly Choices for You and Your Home, by Renee Loux, Rodale, 2008

Eco-Economy, Building an Economy for the Earth, by Lester R. Brown, W.W. Norton & Company, New York London, 2001

Ecological Literacy, Educating Our Children for a Sustainable World, edited by Michael K. Stone and Zenobia Barlow, Sierra Club Books, San Francisco, 2005

Edgar Cayce's Story of Jesus, by Jeffrey Furst, The Berkely Publishing Group, 1976

Egyptian Book Of The Dead, originally translated by Karl Richard Lepsius, 1842, also translated by E.A. Wallis Budge

Estrogen in birth control diminishes sex organs in male rats, by E. Mathews, T.D. Braden, C.S. Williams, J.W. Williams, O. Bolden-Tiller and H.O. Goyal, *Environmental Health News,* January 15, 2010 (also in Toxicological Sciences 112(2):331-343 2010.)

Exploring Reincarnation: The Classic Guide to the Evidence for Past Life Experience, by Hans TenDem, Arkana, 1990

Finance As Warfare, by Michael Hudson, World Economics Association Books and College Publications, 2015

Fish Devastated by Sex Changing Chemicals in Municipal Wastewater, by Dr. Karen Kidd, University of New Brunswick and the Canadian River Institute, 2008

For the Common Good: Redirecting the Economy Toward Community, the Environment and a Sustainable Future, by Herman Daly, Ph.D. and John B. Cobb, Jr., PhD, Beacon Press, 1994

FoxFire, edited by Eliot Wigginton, Doubleday & Co., 1972-2015, (this is a series of 12 books that carry Foxfire in their title. The subject is Appalachia and sustainable early American crafts and skills)

Fuel On Fire, Oil and Politics in Occupied Iraq, by Greg Muttitt, Random House (in USA by New Press) 2011

Getting Us Into War, by Porter Edward Sargent, P. Sargent, 1941

Give and Take, a Revolutionary Approach to Success, by Adam Grant, Viking (the Penguin Group) 2013

Holy Bible, Authorized The King James Version, World Bible Publishers, Inc.

Holy Bible From the Ancient Eastern Text, George M. Lamsa's Translation from the Aramaic of the Peshitta, HarperSanFrancisco, 1933 and 1968

Identifying and Harvesting Edible and Medicinal Plants in Wild (and not so wild) Places, by Steve Brill, with Evelyn Dean, HarperCollins Publisher, 1994

Inventing Reality: The Politics of News Media, by Michael Parenti, St. Martin's Press, 1993

JPS Hebrew-English Tanakh, The Traditional Hebrew Text and the New JPS Translation – Second Edition, The Jewish Publication Society, 1999

Life After Life, by Raymond Moody, M.D., Mockingbird Books, 1975

Measuring the Correlates of War, by J. David Singer and Paul F. Diehl, University of Michigan Press, 1990

Megamedia Shakeout, by Kevin Maney, John Wiley & Sons, Inc., 1995

Molecules of Emotion: The Science Behind Body-Mind Medicine, by Candace Pert, Ph.D., Touchstone, 1997

Nanoparticles – A Thoracic Toxicology Perspective, by Rodger Duffin, Nicholas L. Mills and Ken Donaldson, Yonsie Medical Journal, August 2007

Neurosciences: From Molecule to Behavior – a university textbook, by C. Giovanni Golizia and Pierre-Marie Liedo, Springer Spektrum, Berlin, Heidelberg, 2013

No More Throwaway People: The Coproduction Imperative, by Edgar Cohn, Essential Books, 2000

Only One Earth, the care and maintenance of a small planet, by Barbara Ward and René Dubos, W.W. Norton & Company, Inc., New York, 1972

On the Origins of War and the Preservation of Peace, by Donald Kagan, Doubleday, 1995

Other Lives, Other Selves: A Jungian Psychotherapist Discovers Past Lives, by Roger J. Woolger, Ph.D., Bantam Books, 1988

Children's Exposure to Marijuana – A Guide For Parents, Kristina Dakis, et. al., Great Lakes Center for Children's Environmental Health, Pediatric Environmental Health Specialty Units, December 2018

Phases of Economic Growth, 1850-1973, Kondratieff Waves and Kuznet Swings, by Solomos Solomou, Cambridge University Press, 1987

Plastic Free: How I Kicked the Plastic Habit, by Beth Terry, Skyhorse Publishing, 2015

Prenatal Exposure to Diethyistilbestrol (DES) in Males and Gender-Related Disorders: Results from a 5-Year Study, by Scott P. Kerlin, Ph.D..DES Sons International Network, International Behavioral Development Symposium 2005, in Minot, North Dakota.

Post-Capitalism: A Guide To Our Future, by Paul Mason, London Penguin Books, 2016

Prosperity Without Growth: Economics for a Finite Planet, by Tim Jackson, Abingdon, Oxon, 2017

Rig Veda, a compilation of ancient Hindu religious songs and sayings

Scapegoats: a Defense of Kimmel and Short at Pearl Harbor, by Edward L. Beach, Naval Institute Press, 1995

Scientists: harmful hormones from birth control pills can't be filtered out in sewage treatment, by Thaddeus Baklinski, LifeSiteNews, September 12, 2012.

Secondhand Marijuana Smoke and Kids, Claire McCarthy, M.D., Senior Faculty Editor Harvard Health Publishing, June 5, 1918

Silent Spring, by Rachel Carson, Houghton Mifflin Company Boston, 1960

Small Business For Dummies, by Eric Tyson and Jim Schell, John Wiley & Sons, 2008

Steady State Economics, by Herman Daly, Ph.D., Island Press, 1991

Steering Business Toward Sustainability, by Fritjof Capra and Gunter Pauli, United Nations University Press, 1995

The Analects of Confucius, translated by Simon Leys, W.W. Norton & Company, Inc., copyright by Pierre Ryckmans, 1997

The Best Enemy Money Can Buy, by Anthony Sutton, Liberty House, 1986

The Book of Eights, attributed to Gautama Siddhartha

The Buddha before Buddhism: Wisdom from the early teachings, by Gil Fronsdal, Shambhala, 2016

The Creator and the Cosmos: How the Latest Scientific Discoveries of the Century Reveal God, by Hugh Ross, Ph.D., Nav Press Publishing Group, 1993

The Doctrine Of The Upanisads And The Early Buddha, translated by Shridhor B. Shrotri, Motilal Banasidass Publishers, Pvt. Ltd., Delhi, 1951

The Everything Green Living Book, by Diane Gow McDilda, Adams Media, F+W Publications, 2007

The Greatest Story Ever Sold, The Decline and Fall of Truth in Bush's America, by Frank Kelly Rich, Penguin Press, 2006

The Herb Book, by John Lust, N.D., D.B.M., Bantam Books, 1974

The Historical Dictionary of Hinduism, New Edition, by Jeffery D. Long, The Scarecrow Press, Inc., subsidiary of The Rowman & Littlefield Publishing Group, Inc., 2011

The Hutterites in North America, by Rod Janzen and Max Stanton, The Johns Hopkins University Press, 2010

The Interlinear Greek-English New Testament, with lexicon by George Ricker Berry, Baker Books, a Division of Baker, Book House Co., Twenty-Second printing, 1999

The Interpreter's Bible, Abingdon Press, 1952

The New Jerusalem Bible, Doubleday & Company, Inc., 1985 edition.

The Pharmacopedia of the People's Republic of China, by the China Food and Drug Administration, 2015, usp.org

The Physiology of Mind-Body Interactions, by Gregg D. Jacobs, Ph.D., Journal of Alternative and Complementary Medicine, Vol. 7, Supplement 1, 2001, pp 83-92

The President's War: The Story of the Tonkin Gulf Resolution and How the Nation Was Trapped in Vietnam, by Anthony Austin, Lippincott, 1971

The Religion And Philosophy Of The Veda And Upanishads, by Arthur Berriedale Keith, Greenwood Press, Publishers, 1925 and 1971

The Scientific American Special Issue: The Science of Being Human – Humans: Why We're Unlike Any Other Species on the Planet, Editor-in-Chief Mariette DiChristina, September 2018

The Vietnam Wars 1945-1990, by Marilyn B. Young, Harper Collins, 1991

The Wheel of Life: A Memoir of Living and Dying, by Elisabeth Kubler-Ross, M.D., Touchstone (Simon & Schuster, Inc.) 1997

The Word of the Buddha, from the Pali canon, translated by Nyanatiloka Mahathera, Colombo, 1927

The World's Religions, A Guide To Our Wisdom Traditions, by Houston Smith, HarperSanFrancisco, a Division of HarperCollinsPublishers, 1991

This is Your Brain on Music: the science of a human obsession, by Daniel J. Levitin, a Plume book (Penguin Group) 2007

Time Dollars: The New Currency that Enables Americans to Turn Their Hidden Resource – Time – into Personal Security and Community Renewal, by Edgar Cohn, Rodale, 1992

To Build A Wall: American Jews and the Separation of Church and State (Constitutionalism and Democracy) by Gregg Ivers, University of Virginia Press, 1995

Total War: Causes and Courses of the Second World War, by Peter Calvocoressi and Guy Wint, Penguin Press, 1972

Truth is the First Casualty: The Gulf of Tonkin Affair: Illusion and Reality, by Joseph C. Goulden, Rand McNally, 1969

Upanisads, translated by T.M.P. Mahadevan, Published by Arnold Heinemann, 1975

War, a Cruel Necessity? Edited by Robert A. Hinde and Helen E. Watson, St. Martin's Press, 1994

War Cycles, Peace Cycles, the necessity for war in modern finance, by Richard Kelly Hoskins, the Virginia Publishing Company, 1985

War in the World System, edited by Richard K. Schaeffer, Emory University, 1988

Where Reincarnation and Biology Intersect, by Ian Stevenson, M.D., Praeger Publishers, 1997

Why Your Child is Hyperactive, by Ben Feingold, M.D., Random House, 1974

Made in the USA
Middletown, DE
06 August 2023

36149495R00050